HELP! I TITHE BUT I'M STILL BROKE!

Unless otherwise indicated, all Scripture quotations are taken from the King James Version (KJV) of the Bible.

Scripture quotations marked NLT are taken from the Holy Bible, New Living Translation, © 1996. Used by permission of Tyndale House Publishers, Inc., Wheaton, Illinois 60189. All rights reserved.

Scripture quotations marked NKJV are taken from the New King James Version, © 1979, 1980, 1982 by Thomas Nelson, Inc. Used by permission. All rights reserved.

What Key Estate Planning Tools Should I Know About?, How Can My Charity and I Both Benefit from My Gift?, What Gifting Strategies Are Available To Me?, and How Can I Benefit From a Wealth Replacement Trust? are from Emerald Publications, © 2006, Emerald Publications. Used by permission.

Hakeem J. Webb, MSFS, RIS
National Christian Financial Advisors, Inc.
49 Leavenworth Street, Suite 305
Waterbury, CT 06702
Telephone: 203.757.7907
Web site: www.ncfallc.com
Email: hjw@ncfallc.com

Edited by: Bill Wilson and Diane James

Order this book online at www.trafford.com/07-1019
or email orders@trafford.com

Most Trafford titles are also available at major online book retailers.

Note for Librarians: A cataloguing record for this book is available from Library and Archives Canada at www.collectionscanada.ca/amicus/index-e.html

ISBN: 978-1-4251-2899-9

We at Trafford believe that it is the responsibility of us all, as both individuals and corporations, to make choices that are environmentally and socially sound. You, in turn, are supporting this responsible conduct each time you purchase a Trafford book, or make use of our publishing services. To find out how you are helping, please visit www.trafford.com/responsiblepublishing.html

Our mission is to efficiently provide the world's finest, most comprehensive book publishing service, enabling every author to experience success. To find out how to publish your book, your way, and have it available worldwide, visit us online at www.trafford.com/10510

www.trafford.com

North America & international
toll-free: 1 888 232 4444 (USA & Canada)
phone: 250 383 6864 • fax: 250 383 6804
email: info@trafford.com

The United Kingdom & Europe
phone: +44 (0)1865 722 113 • local rate: 0845 230 9601
facsimile: +44 (0)1865 722 868 • email: info.uk@trafford.com

10 9 8 7 6 5 4 3 2

A CHRISTIAN GUIDE TO FINANCIAL PLANNING

Finance is all Greek to me and that's how, I believe, the majority of the Body of Christ feels today. HELP! I TITHE BUT I'M STILL BROKE! helped give me a few new handles as I move my way through the world of finance. May the Lord continue to bless you as you consider future writing projects with other areas of finance especially, INSURANCE!
- Pastor Pat Hail, Jr., Sola Scriptura Ministries, Inc.

I was pleased as I read HELP! I TITHE BUT I'M STILL BROKE! and see the chapter on Moral Investing. God's word tells us in 2 Corinthians 6:17 (NKJV) Therefore "Come out from among them And be separate, says the Lord. Do not touch what is unclean. And I will receive." I appreciated the emphasis Hakeem placed on this area of Investing; along with his other points on Christian financial planning, this perspective was very insightful.
- Dave Hart, Vice President, Broker/Dealer Relations, The Timothy Plan

Hakeem J. Webb is a regular on our live radio program Living Christian KCIS AM 630 and brings the same wisdom and enthusiasm to his book, "HELP! I TITHE BUT I'M STILL BROKE! A CHRISTIAN GUIDE TO FINANCIAL PLANNING." A straight forward look at questions all of us should know the answers to, but are sometimes afraid to admit we don't. EVERYONE will learn something from this book and EVERYONE can learn from its pages if they put these principles into practice.
- Michelle Mendoza, host Living Christian

Hakeem thank you for allowing me to read your book. It is well-thought out and thorough in its approach to guiding one through the maze of their finances. I found it to have sound Biblical application and explanation of how the Bible applies to one's finances and how one should handle their finances in accordance to scripture.

I learned quite a bit from your book. I especially liked your Financial Reversal Cycle. It is human nature to worry in time of financial strife, and this visual and written explanation of how finances become reversed was simple, yet powerful.

The Financial Vitamins made a lot of sense to me. Just as we care for our health and bodies with Vitamins daily, so, too, we should care for our finances and financial mind by reading scriptures and taking our Financial Vitamins daily. This made me feel empowered over my finances.

There are many other points that I enjoyed---Many other points too numerous to name, but in all, a stellar book that is a great guide and handbook.
- Maggie Valle, Producer Living Christian

CONTENTS

Riches and honour are with me;
yea, durable riches and righteouseness.
My fruit is better than gold, yea,
than fine gold; and my revenue than
choice silver.
I lead in the way of righteousness,
in the midst of the paths of judgment;
That I may cause those that love
me to inherit substance; and I will fill
their treasures.

Proverbs 8:18-21 (KJV)

HELP! I TITHE BUT I'M STILL BROKE!

A CHRISTIAN GUIDE TO FINANCIAL PLANNING

Hakeem J. Webb, MSFS

Disclaimer

The thoughts and opinions of the author as expressed in this book are not the thoughts or opinions of any company with whom the author of the book may be associated, including any broker-dealer or investment adviser registered under state or federal law.

This book is not an advertisement for securities brokerage or investment advisory services. Though the author of this book has or may provide securities brokerage and investment advisory services to the public, the purpose of this book is to provide the views of the author and general information only -- not specific investment advice to any reader. This book does not provide securities brokerage or investment advisory services or advertise any services provided by the author.

This book has not been reviewed by state or federal authorities, and the content has not been approved by any regulatory body.

Nothing herein is to be construed as an offer or a solicitation of an offer to buy or sell any security.

The Beginning of The Call

> For I know the thoughts that I think toward you, saith the Lord, thoughts of peace, and not of evil, to give you an expected end.
>
> Jeremiah 29:11

Growing up, I did not hear money mentioned in church except as the root of all evil. Not even when there was a financial need, such as the building fund, burial of a church member who did not have any insurance, or when church bills were due. Nobody dared use the word "money"; they would use the word, ***offering.*** The discussion would go something like this: "The church has to meet the deadline for the building fund so we are going to take up a special *offering.*" "Sister Mary's husband died and we would like to take up a special *offering.*" Or, "The roof on the church building is in need of repair and we are asking that everyone give extra in the *offering.*" To this day, there are some churches that still don't dare mention money during the service, especially not in the sanctuary.

When I received Jesus as my Lord and Savior and decided to serve Him with all my heart, I had just started working for one of the world's largest financial services companies.

When asked what I did for a living, I replied, "I'm a financial consultant. I help people save for retirement, fund their children's education, invest in the stock market, and protect their families in the event of an unexpected death." Surprisingly to me, I found that most, if not all, did not have a clue of what I was talking about.

One evening during a young men's study and prayer group meeting, a brother seemed to have an attitude towards me and stated, "You know brother Hakeem, rich people cannot get into heaven." I looked around the room and all I could see on the faces of all the men and hear was, "Yes, that's true." The only exceptions were the minister who was teaching and a man who owned his own construction company. To complicate matters, I dressed well and had plenty money in the bank. Nevertheless, at that time in my walk I didn't know what to say because I was a babe in Christ.

At the end of the meeting I went to the teacher and said, "I will not be back next week." He asked why and I responded, "I just heard I am not going to be able to get into heaven." He asked, "Are you rich?" I said, "No, not right now, but I am sure on my way." He said, "Don't let what you heard keep you from coming back next week. In the meantime, read **Deuteronomy 8:18** and **Proverbs 10:22.**" He also called me during the week and said, "Hakeem, God has a plan for you and He is going to use you to teach us and the body of Christ how to handle money for the Kingdom." I thought he was just saying that to get me to come back, but from that point to the present, that's exactly what I've been doing.

I read the Scriptures, received encouragement, spoke with the teacher during the week and went back the following week. The teacher told me of the Full Gospel Business Men's Fellowship International. God supernaturally blessed me by opening an opportunity to become a life-time member of this organization for only $100 dollars. In addition, the teacher, his brother, and the pastor took a special interest in helping me in my spiritual growth by teaching me the Word of God in what seemed like daily feedings.

I later found out that the gentleman who made the statement, as well as some other group members, have done this before and caused many new believers to leave the church. In fact, this was one of the reasons the church was in financial trouble and on the verge of having its partially built cultural center foreclosed.

That year, God used me to reach out and witness to a large number of men. I assisted the pastor with the men's group, teaching them the true Word of God and seeing the group grow from a few men to about a hundred. As a group, the Lord raised us up to become the biggest givers in the church. He also used me during a church meeting, which was held to receive an offering for the cultural center. And yes, I announced the exact amount that was needed and sowed what was, at that time, my largest financial seed ever.

The good report is, the church raised the money, the center was built, and to this day it remains a beacon of light in the South Bronx of New York.

The sad part of this story is that the poor gentleman who originally wanted me to identify with his poverty did not know I grew up poor and that God was responsible for getting me out. He also did not know that I asked God back in the fifth grade to keep me from being poor, and that in return I promised Him that I would teach others.

From that point to present, I have been blessed by God financially and the Lord continues to use me to help people come out of debt, invest and manage their money from a biblical perspective, and achieve financial freedom.

Introduction

Positioning The Body of Christ To Receive Her Inheritance

> And if you are untrustworthy about worldly wealth, who will trust you with the true riches of heaven?
>
> Luke 16:11 (NLT)

The book you are reading is Volume 1, "Help! I Tithe But I'm Still Broke!" from the Money, Success and Wealth Series™. It is by no means an exhaustive guide on financial planning, which would take hundreds, if not thousands, of pages and many years of study. However, I think, it's one of the best, if not the only, Christian financial books that combines both spiritual and practical principles in the financial planning process.

I pray this book will help guide you in managing God's and your finances. The principles taught in this book are principles that my wife and I live by. Personally, I've been able to use these principles to go from poverty to prosperity; from having no money to owning a full-service financial firm that generates millions of dollars in sales with over 400 clients throughout the world; from growing up being evicted multiple times as a child to now finalizing plans to build our 8,000 square foot dream home.

The good news--if God did it for me, He is willing and able to do it for you if you are willing to hear, learn and apply to your everyday life the principles taught within these pages.

I must disclose at the onset that this book is specifically written to Christians, meaning those who have been redeemed from the curse of the law. You are wondering about the curse, what it is and which books are under the law. Genesis, Exodus, Leviticus, Numbers and Deuteronomy are the first five books of the law. The curse entered the earth realm after Adam fell because of disobedience. The penalty for breaking the law found in these books is the curse.

A real intimate look at the curse can be found in **Deuteronomy 28:15-68.** Most of us in the Body of Christ always want to know about the blessings, which is good. I put before you today, however, that if you can recognize or identify the curse, then seek the Lord and His word for the answer, you will surely be on your way toward the blessings. Whenever any one of these curses tries to enter your thoughts or show up in your life, just remind the devil that you've been redeemed and speak the blessings that you want over your situation.

"Christ hath redeemed us from the curse of the law, being made a curse for us; for it is written, Cursed is every one that hangeth on a tree: That the blessing of Abraham might come on the Gentiles through Jesus Christ..."

Galatians 3:13-14

Many Christians today find themselves lacking money or resources to adequately sustain themselves. Some maintain an overwhelming level of debt that makes them feel trapped. Others find that when their income increases, their expenses also increase, diminishing their rise in earnings. All of this is part of the curse and should not be the lifestyle of the believer.

We were not only redeemed from the curse, we were also promised to receive wealth and riches. Few of us are living such a life. So, I hope this book will position the Body of Christ for Her inheritance.

If you discover this book and you aren't a Christian, hopefully you'll find some principles to live by. Some may not work because you aren't a Christian yet, but following them may help you uncover God's true nature, for He loves you and gave His only begotten son Jesus Christ so you could begin a path of life that promises you abundance.

In order to receive this life, go to the back of this book and read aloud the salvation prayer. If you are sincere and believe in your heart what you read and said, then you will become part of the family of God and immediately be granted access and benefit from these promises.

To better understand this, you first would have to understand that the Bible is not addressing everyone in the world indiscriminately. Ultimately it does, but you have to determine which part of the Bible is addressing you, or "us", because the Bible speaks to three groups of people:

1. **Sinners** – A person who hasn't accepted God's plan of salvation. Sinners, not because of what they do or how they live, but because they haven't accepted God's plan of Salvation.
2. **Christians** – Someone who has accepted God's plan of Salvation. This is done by accepting and receiving His son, Jesus Christ, as your Lord and Savior.
3. **Jews** – (Israel) God's chosen people.

Somewhere along the line, after the first church was established in the Book of Acts, the devil tricked some believers into thinking lack and poverty were humble and, therefore, made you closer to God. This is a lie. The word of the Lord lets us know, **"It is not the decreed will of God to let any of his children be poor!"**

2 Corinthians 8:9 For ye know the grace of our Lord Jesus Christ, that though he was rich, yet for your sakes he became poor, that you through his poverty might be rich.

John 10:10 The thief cometh not, but for to steal, and to kill, and to destroy: I am come (Jesus Christ) that they might have life, and that they might have it more abundantly.

However, if you let yourself be poor, God will honor your desire. Further, we are not all God's children, as some will have you to believe. Only those who have accepted Jesus as their Lord and Savior are God's children, but we all are His creation, which is different.

Another truth that you need to know and settle in your heart is that when you are in Christ and "knowledgeable" of what that means, then you are out of the scope of the curse. The curse, therefore, has no legal right over your life.

Before you decide whether you are under the curse of poverty, you should know what is considered poor. Being poor means to lack substance--that is, the money or resources needed to adequately sustain oneself. You must also ask yourself, "Are people poor because there is not enough money in the world?"

The answer is **"no."** People are poor because they have not learned how to appropriate money or resources of tangible value into their lives, or they have not been taught what to ask for or how to get into position to receive.

The Bible clearly states what we should do first before we even ask. However, if you fail to seek Him you will not find Him. And if you fail to seek the Kingdom of God first, which is His way of doing things, you will also fail. After you first seek His Kingdom, He will teach and direct you to the next place to seek or the next steps to take.

But seek ye first the kingdom of God, and his righteousness and all these things shall be added unto you.

Matthew 6:33

In addition, if you don't ask, He can't answer! And if you don't ask the right questions, then you won't get the right answers for your situation. To do this, you will have to spend some quality time with Father God.

Ask, and it shall be given you, seek, and ye shall find, knock and it shall be opened unto you.

Matthew 7:7

Now, before you read the rest of this book, you must settle in your heart and mind that you are supposed to be rich, knowing that Jesus paid the price for your poverty, lack, insufficiency and financial containment just as much as he paid the price for your sin debt. It's all about our salvation package.

I know this may be a tough statement for some of you to believe because you probably have never heard this before. Nevertheless, when you first heard about being Spirit-filled, with evidence of speaking in tongues, you probably doubted and asked yourself if it were true.

In fact, when most people hear that Healing is for all, and God wants you to be well, they shake their heads and say, "No way!"

Child of God, if you have to take a moment and pray and ask Jesus to help your unbelief, please do so, because neither Jesus nor I want you to miss this revelation. Take a look at the word of God:

For ye know the grace of our Lord Jesus Christ that though he was rich, yet for your sakes he became poor, that ye through his poverty might be rich.

2 Corinthians 8: 9

Okay, you're scratching your head saying, **"How do I become rich through poverty?"** Again, you must understand that **"poverty" and "rich" are relative words!**

For example, Bill Gates, the richest man in the world, at least for now, may consider Donald Trump to be poor. Bill Gates is a multi-billionaire, while Donald Trump has only several billion dollars. Conversely, Donald Trump may consider the Rapper Jay-Z to be poor because Jay-Z has several million dollars compared to his several billion. You see, it is all relative.

With that, understand Jesus left Heaven to come to the earth. The moment he entered this realm He became poor, regardless of the fact that He received gold, frankincense and other valuable spices. He lived where the streets are paved with pure gold, the building of the wall of it was jasper; and the city was pure gold, like unto clear glass; and the twelve gates were twelve pearls. **(Revelation 21:10-21)**.

To grasp what I mean, allow me to translate what the value of the golden streets alone would be worth:

The street was 1,500 miles long, 24 feet wide and 2 feet deep. In ounces, as gold is measured, that would be 2 quadrillion, 785 trillion, 89 billion, 871 million, 872 thousand, conservatively in today's dollars, or $2,785,089,871,872,000. And that's just the streets! That is shouting news right there! So never again take the thought or lie from the devil that you should be poor, or in lack or barely getting by. When that thought comes up, use these two scriptures, **2 Corinthians 8:9 and Revelations 21:10-21,** to cast it down. Then shout, **"I am the RICH protecting my RICHES!"**

So turn the page and begin reading the only book that I am aware of that will teach you both spiritual and natural principles that will position you to receive wealth. After all, it's been laid up for us for over 2,000 years. And it's time to **RECEIVE IT!**

PROSPERITY OF GOD'S PEOPLE

Abraham	"And Abram was very rich in cattle, in silver, and in gold."	Gen. 13:2
Isaac	"The man became rich, and his wealth continued to grow until he became very wealthy."	Gen. 26:13, NIV
Jacob	"Thus the man increased and became exceedingly rich, and had many sheep and goats, and maidservants, camels, and donkeys."	Gen. 30:43, TAB
Joseph	Second in command to the Pharaoh, ruler over Egypt, the first known and recorded commodity, currency trader and real estate broker. In short, Joseph was an anointed financial minister. It is also safe to say he established what easily could be classified as the first exchange. "But the Lord was with Joseph, and he (though a slave) was a prosperous Man…"	Gen. 39:2 TAB Gen. 41:40-44
Moses and the children of Israel	Left Egypt with the wealth and riches of Egypt. "The Israelites did according to the word of Moses; and they (urgently) asked of the Egyptians jewels of silver and of gold, and clothing. The Lord gave the people favor in the sight of the Egyptians (of those things)."	Ex. 12:35-33 36, TAB
David	"He died in a good old age (his seventy-first year) full and satisfied with days, riches and honor;"	1 Chron. 29:28, TAB
Solomon	Richest man who ever lived. "I will also give you wealth, riches and honor, such as no king who was before you ever had and none after you will have."	2 Chron. 1:12, NIV 1 Kings 10:23
Jehoshaphat	"Therefore the Lord established the kingdom in his hand and all Judah brought tribute to Jehoshaphat, and he had great riches and honor."	2 Chron.17:5, TAB

PROSPERITY OF GOD'S PEOPLE, CONTINUED

Job	Greatest man in the east. "He possessed seven thousand sheep, three thousand camels, five hundred yoke of oxen, five hundred female donkeys, and a very great body of servants, so that this man was the greatest of all the men of the east." Job 1:3, TAB
Daniel	Ruler over Babylon. "Then the king made Daniel great, and gave Him many great gifts, and made him to rule over the whole Province of Babylon, and to be chief governor over all the wise Men of Babylon." "So this man Daniel prospered in the reign of Darius and in the reign of Cyrus the Persian." Dan. 2:48; 6:28
Joseph of Arimathea	"As evening approached, there came a rich man from Arimathea, named Joseph, who had himself become a disciple of Jesus." Matt. 27:57, NIV
Cornelius	Roman Centurion. "There was a certain man in Caesarea called Cornelius, a centurion of the band called Italian band. A devout man, and one that feared God with all his house, which gave much alms to the people, and prayed to God always." Acts 10:1-2
Lydia	Dealer of purple cloth. "One of those listening was a woman named Lydia, a dealer in purple cloth from the city of Thyatira, who was a worshiper of God." Acts 16:14, NIV
Believers in the Early Church	"There were no needy persons among them. For from time to time those who owned lands or houses sold them, brought the money from the sales and put it at the apostles' feet, and it was distributed to anyone as he had need." Acts 4:34-35, NIV

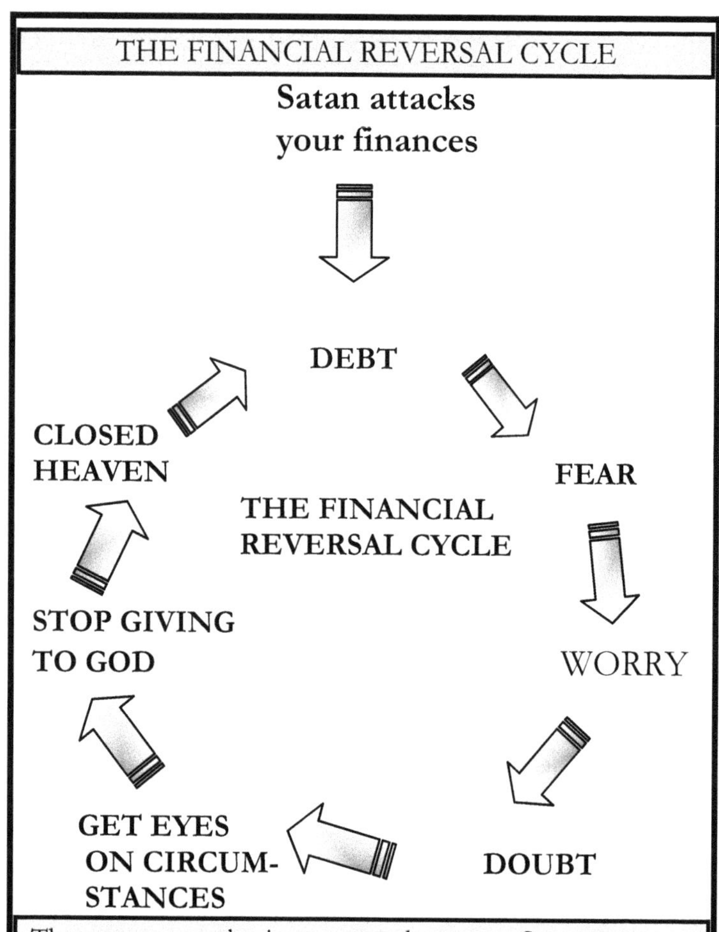

The moment you begin to worry about your finances, you open yourself up for the financial reversal cycle! Satan will try to fill your mind with fear, worry and doubt. And, if you keep your eyes on your circumstances, you will stop giving to God which will block the flow of God's provision in your life. To break out of the financial reversal cycle, cast out all fear, worry and doubt, get your eyes off your circumstances, continue to give to God, expecting, believing and trusting Him to fulfill His promises to you.

Chapter 1

YOUR BARNS SHALL BE FILLED WITH PLENTY

> Honour the Lord with thy substance, and with the firstfruits of all thine increase; So shall thy barns (bank or brokerage) accounts be filled with plenty, and thy presses (wallets or purses) shall burst out with new wine.
>
> Proverbs 3:9

There are many Christians today who are frustrated, and don't understand why they are not reaping God's promises of blessing and prosperity. They are claiming His promises, but they are not following the principles and plans that God set up about giving. Because of not honoring God with their substance, they are not benefiting from God's promises. God prospers and blesses us as we honor Him with the wealth He has placed in our hands.

Regardless of your income or what you have, whether it is a large or small amount, God expects you to honor Him with it.

The word "plenty" in the verse above means "fullness; abundance." The Hebrew root word is "to become satisfied." The expression "so shall thy barns be filled with plenty" depicts the greatest possible abundance.

When we honor the Lord with our substance, God promises to not only supply our needs, but to bless us with PLENTY…the greatest possible ABUNDANCE. Are you ready for God to bless you with the greatest possible abundance?

We do not have the right, and cannot expect to reap God's blessings, if we are not faithful in our giving to God and the work of ministry. This may be hard for some people to accept, but it is true. We cannot expect God to deliver us out of financial bondage, and to prosper and bless us when we fail to be a good steward of what God has given us. Tithing does not mean you are a good steward; it means you are obedient and trust God and His financial system. What you do with the offerings and the rest of the money will decide if you are a good steward or not. The tithe is just the beginning of what I refer to as "Christian Covenant Membership." As believers we must go beyond this point to receive the wealth of the Word. We must manage the rest that God allows us to keep by giving to the poor, contributing to world evangelism, saving, investing and doing business.

Jesus put it this way, **"Occupy 'till I come"**, Luke 19:13. The Greek word for occupy is *"Pragmateuomai"* (Strong concordance number 4231), which means (1) to be occupied in anything, (2) to carry on a business, or (3) to carry on the business of a banker or a trader.

If you continue reading Luke 19 verses 15-27, you will see the reward of those who went out and gained interest by trading and doing business with the Lord's money. He made them rulers over "CITIES." Most churches are confessing that they are going to take over cities, but never do, and yet Jesus himself gives us the principle of how to receive cities. When we are not following His instructions, frustration continues to mount.

Conversely, the servant who dug a hole for what he received ended up having the money taken from him and it was given to the one who increased what was given to him.

In other words, the good servant earned the greatest potential return available and did not allow the fear of risk to grip him to do nothing. In the end, we see that the words of the bad servant and the lack of relationship with Jesus cost him everything, including his eternal life in heaven.

And I was afraid I would lose your money, so I hid it in the earth and here it is! "But the master replied, "You wicked and lazy servant! You think I'm a hard man, do you, harvesting crops I didn't plant and gathering crops I didn't cultivate? Well, you should at least have put my money into the bank so I would have some interest. Now throw this useless servant into outer darkness, where there will be weeping and gnashing of teeth.

Matthew 25:25-27, 30
(NLT)

This teaching was one of the first revelations God gave me about financial breakthroughs. The other point you must realize is that animals and cattle represented wealth. Unless you are raising cattle, you probably do not have a barn, but you should have a bank account, brokerage account, wallets or purses. In fact, if you really believe God is going to give you the greatest possible abundance, then you will prepare to receive it by having not just one bank account, but two or three. After all, banks can only insure your holdings up to $100,000 FDIC.

FEAR NOT!

"For God hath not given us the spirit of fear; but of power, and of love, and of a sound mind."
2 Timothy 1:7

RISK OF INVESTING

All investments contain some risk, and it's possible to lose money in any investment. Below are a few of those risks with some basic information about each. However, before reviewing, let me say that risk is another word for "fear". Risk is associated with the possible chance of losing money, and as a result, some people decide not to invest or invest little because they "fear" having less than they started out with. But let an adviser guarantee that they will not lose any money and their desire to invest changes. Most people won't hesitate to invest or place their money into an account like that.

For example, banks with their CDs and government bonds are considered safe investments attracting millions in assets. Therefore, I think, risk is another form of "fear", and since it's "fear", we as believers shouldn't tolerate any form of "fear" based on Romans 8:15 which tells us, "For ye have not received the spirit of bondage again to fear; but ye have received the spirit of adoption, whereby we cry Abba, Father." This passage of scripture compares "fear" to bondage, and many Christians are in financial bondage because they don't know the truth about risk, or at the very least, they are not increasing the resources God has given them. We also see in 2 Timothy 1:7, "For God hath not given us the spirit of fear; but of power, and of love, and of a sound mind." Don't get me wrong, risks do exist. So I strongly recommend you know and understand all the risk involved before investing your money. Remember, "My people are destroyed for lack of knowledge." (Hosea 4:6)

I am saying most people, if given all the facts and details, are able to make a decision of quality; and as believers, we can add FAITH and trust in God and the Holy Spirit for guidance to lead us into all truths.

To make a decision of quality and uproot the fear of investing, you must have understanding. Therefore, listed below are various types of risk:

- **<u>Market risk</u>** – Your investment principal's value may fluctuate from day to day, as influenced by U.S. or global economic, political and/or social events, or just a change in market psychology. Such reactions may be short-term, and therefore, not indicative of long-term value.

- **Company risk** – The value of each company's stock is affected by current expectations for that company or its industry sector, as well as general market risk.

- **Interest rate risk** – Generally, short-term bond investments are less impacted by interest rate movements than long-term bond investments. Bond values tend to move inversely to interest rates (i.e., when interest rates go up, bond values go down).

- **Credit risk** – Common to bonds, the lower the credit worthiness of your investment, the higher its yield and risk in comparison to investments with a higher credit rating.

- **Inflation (purchasing power risk)** – A representation of the increased cost of living during a given time period, usually measured yearly or monthly.

- **Currency risk** – Certain investments in foreign securities or in securities that invest in foreign investments can be subject to fluctuations because of the value of the dollar relative to the currency of other nations.

- **Securities** – Some securities are prone to greater risk factors. Typically, low-priced securities, newly issued securities, foreign-issued securities, low-rated or unrated fixed income securities and illiquid securities (such as limited partnerships) are considered more speculative in nature than more mature, seasoned companies. Equities are available with all levels of risk and potential reward.

- **Margin accounts** – The use of borrowed funds to finance all or a portion of a purchase of an investment can increase investment returns when an investment increases above the purchase price and the interest cost. However, losses are increased by leverage, materially increasing the risk of investing on margin, as well as increasing the investment's costs. Therefore, only those investors who understand how to place orders with the necessary precautions to limit loss or those capable of sustaining a loss of their entire investment and more, should purchase securities in this manner.

Chapter 2

MONEY

MONEY: ITS PURPOSE

> Wisdom is good with an inheritance and by it there is profit to them that see the sun. For wisdom is a defence and money is a defence...
>
> Ecclesiastes 7:11-12

Before you benefit from money, or anything for that matter, you must first understand its purpose and use. If this is not understood, then it will be misused or abused. For example, a desk is a table frame or case with a sloping or horizontal surface especially used for writing and reading and often with drawers and compartments. Now, if you think a desk is something to eat on or sleep on, the likelihood of enjoying its original benefits are slim to none.

The same applies to money. Its purpose is two-fold:

1. To "Grow" or earn interest
2. To pay for goods and services

Therefore, if you think money's only purpose is to purchase goods and services, you are misusing money and will shortly be without it. Conversely, if you only aim for growing your money and never use it to buy goods and services, you too will eventually end up without.

MONEY: A SHORT HISTORY

Much of financial planning involves money: earning it, spending it and saving it. However, before money there was barter. In the Old World, Roman soldiers were often paid with sacks of salt, giving us the word "salary." In the New World, perhaps the best-known example of barter was when Peter Minuit exchanged $24 worth of trinkets and beads for the island of Manhattan, which has taught us all the importance of understanding true value.

Although a great deal of barter continues throughout the world, barter is inefficient when it comes to paying for goods and services. As early as 2,500 B.C., precious metals began to be used throughout Egypt and Asia Minor. This naturally led to the minting of metals into coins that facilitated the process of exchange, with the value of the coin being determined by the value of the underlying metal (e.g., pound sterling).

The American dollar owes its name to a silver coin called, the *Joachimsthaler,* which was first minted in Bohemia in 1519. Widely circulated throughout Europe, in England it became known as, "the dollar". In the United States, paper money was first issued in varying denominations by the colonies.

To finance the American Revolution, the Continental Congress issued notes that were declared to be redeemable in either gold or silver coins, but these notes eventually became virtually worthless due to the lack of sufficient gold and silver reserves.

Although the federal government first minted silver "dollars" in 1794, it was not until 1863 that a uniform currency was established that replaced the paper money previously issued by local banks.

Today, circulation currency, both paper and coin, is no longer backed by either gold or silver reserves, but rather by the full faith and credit of the United States.

Traditionally, there have been three basic forms of money: currency, coins and checks drawn on banks and other financial firms. To these should be added credit cards, debit cards, and electronic payments (both preauthorized and remote). The following table of consumer payment systems by method of payment suggests that credit cards, debit cards and electronic payments will be increasingly used as a substitute for payment by check.

	Amount $ billions		Percent Distribution	
	2000	2008*	2000	2008*
Cash	1,092	1,152	20.6	15.7
Direct Check Payments	2,271	1,459	42.9	19.8
Credit Cards	1,238	2,178	23.4	29.6
Debit Cards	309	1,213	5.8	16.5
Electronic Payments	219	1,045	4.1	14.2

*** projected**

SAVINGS VEHICLES

Savings generally involve short-term goals with an emphasis on liquidity and safety of principal. In contrast, investing involves longer-term goals with lower liquidity and less safety of principal. For example, funds are saved in short-term interest-bearing debt instruments, such as certificates of deposits or United States Treasury bills (created and transferred in the money market), whereas funds are invested in the longer-term debts or equity, such as corporate bonds or common stocks (created and traded in the capital markets). Unfortunately, in practice the terms are often used interchangeably.

Checking Accounts

Also known as regular checking, these are demand accounts that allow the depositor to issue checks directing the financial institution to pay the party listed on the check a specific sum of money. The credit union version of a checking account is known as a share draft account, and also, in my opinion, is the best place to put your money if you are an individual or family. Provided there are sufficient funds in the account, there are no limitations on the withdrawal.

A regular checking account pays no interest on the account balance. Service charges may be applied, but are often waived if a minimum account balance is maintained or the account holder is over a certain age (the so-called "senior" account).

Both automated teller machines (ATMs) and debit cards have become very popular ways of accessing funds in checking accounts.

NOW Accounts

In contrast to regular checking accounts, the NOW (negotiated order of withdrawal) accounts pay interest on account balances. Many other institution-specific names are used to describe these accounts (e.g., "Check-plus Account"). Although all savings account interest rate ceilings and minimum balance requirements at commercial banks and savings institutions were removed in 1986, most financial institutions impose their own minimum balance limits for interest to be credited, often between $500 and $1,000. Therefore, it will serve you well to investigate where you place your money.

Interest is credited at whatever rate is set by the institution and is typically increased (tiered) if larger balances are maintained (e.g., amounts over $2,500). Since fees will offset interest earned, evaluation of a particular account should include determining exactly what, if any, monthly or other fees are charged. Provided a minimum balance is maintained, monthly fees are often waived. The *dividend bearing share draft account* is the credit union version of a NOW account, and again, I believe the best place for an individual or family to place their money.

Super NOW Accounts

These are NOW accounts that are generally less restrictive than Money Market Deposit Accounts (MMDAs). Interest rates are usually higher than NOW accounts, but less than MMDAs. Tiered interest rates are usually offered. Some accounts charge per item processing fees for checks or deposits, some accounts do not impose these fees, and still other accounts waive these fees, provided a minimum balance is maintained.

Savings Accounts

These accounts, also referred to as "passbook accounts," are considered the most basic of bank savings vehicles. The term "statement account" is often used in reference to savings accounts that record transactions by computer and provide either monthly or quarterly statements in lieu of passbook entries.

In contrast to demand deposits, or checking accounts, savings accounts are also referred to as *time deposits* since the funds are expected to remain on deposit for longer periods. In fact, many accounts stipulate that depositors may be required to wait a stated number of days before receiving payment. However, this requirement is often waived. While funds in a savings account are both safe and liquid, the rates paid on savings accounts are typically the lowest rates offered.

Higher, or tiered, rates of interest are usually paid on larger account balances or for time deposits. It is also worth noting that Internet banking is becoming extremely popular and often offers very attractive rates on savings accounts as a result of not having to pay for the typical overhead found at local institutions with branches.

Money Market Mutual Funds (MMMF)

Also referred to as "Money Market Funds," these funds, issued by investment companies and insurance companies, are handled by mutual fund managers. Shares are purchased at a fixed price of $1 each and form a pool of money that is used to purchase short-term and high-quality debt obligations of government entities, commercial banks, and corporations (e.g., Treasury bills, bank certificate of deposits, and corporate commercial paper). MMMFs are sold as no load funds (i.e., no sales commission), but management fees are charged. Although earnings are technically dividends, they are taxed as interest income.

Because the securities purchased are of very high denominations, MMMFs are able to obtain the highest rates available on the market. The interest rates change daily due to the fluctuating nature of the fund's portfolio of debt instruments.

The minimum initial investment and check writing privileges vary from one account to another. Typically, checks must be for a minimum amount, varying from $250 to $500.

Although not insured by the FDIC, if purchased from a brokerage firm, MMMFs are considered securities and are insured against the bankruptcy of the firm by the Securities Investor Protection Corporation (SIPC), but they are not insured against a loss stemming from the underlying investments. However, because of their short-term nature and high quality, most experts regard them about as safe as commercial paper (commercial paper is unsecured, short-term debt instruments issued by banks and corporations in order to meet immediate cash needs).

Money Market Deposit Accounts (MMDA)

These accounts, also referred to as "Money Market Accounts," were developed by financial institutions in order to compete against the Money Market Mutual Funds (MMMF) offered by investment and insurance companies. Interest is market-based, meaning that the rate will vary from week to week. Although the interest rates are generally lower than those available with an MMMF, they offer two advantages not enjoyed by the MMMF: the convenience of a local bank or savings association, and the safety of being federally insured (up to $100,000). A minimum balance is required, and withdrawals by check or electronic transfer are usually very limited in number, with fees charged for any excess number of withdrawals (e.g., more than three per month). Because of these fees, MMDAs are more similar in nature to savings accounts than checking accounts.

Certificates Of Deposit (CD)

Certificates of deposit are issued by commercial banks, savings and loan associations, savings banks and credit unions. The most common maturity periods range from three months to five years. Because funds are being committed for a longer period of time, the rate of return earned on CDs is typically higher than those offered on savings accounts and money market instruments. However, if the funds are withdrawn prior to maturity, a *penalty* in the form of forfeited interest is assessed (e.g., three month's interest).

Tiered rates are typically offered, with higher rates for longer terms and larger amounts. Because rates can differ substantially from one region of the country to another, it is wise to shop around for the best rate. The Wall Street Journal and Internet are good sources for researching rates. Higher yields can also be obtained from brokered CDs. These are larger denomination bank CDs ($1,000 and up) that are purchased through brokers who shop nationally for the highest available rates. The bank pays commissions for brokered CDs. Unlike the typical CD, the funds in brokered CDs can often be assessed early and without a bank-imposed penalty by having a broker sell them in the secondary markets.

Rising interest rates will depress the value of a fixed-rate CD. Laddering can be an effective way of providing some protection against falling interest rates. By laddering, I mean determine what amount of your money is needed in three months, six months, a year, etc., and then split the amounts among the CDs accordingly.

Another type of CD is the hybrid. Although rates are typically fixed, this CD offers variable rates tied to a specific market index (e.g., the S&P 500). Because the frequency with which interest is compounded is an important determinant of a CD's return, it is important to determine the yield, not just the interest rate.

While the vast majority of CDs are issued by institutions insured by the FDIC, it is always important to verify that a CD is federally insured.

ANNUAL PERCENTAGE YIELD (APY)

This is the effective, or true, annual rate of return earned in an interest-bearing account or instrument, expressed as a percentage. It takes into consideration the effect of compounding. When the APY is higher than the declared interest rate, the interest is compounded (i.e., interest is being paid on interest). For example, if $1,000 placed in a CD paying 5% interest (compounded monthly) earns $51.16 during the period April 1 to the following March 31, the APY is 5.116%. If interest were compounded quarterly, the APY would be 5.095% and the interest earned would by $50.95. If the interest were not compounded, the interest earned would be only $50.00 (i.e., simple versus compounded interest).

PAYMENT CARDS (PLASTIC)

Credit Cards

Credit cards generally include any card that is repeatedly used to borrow money or buy goods on credit. They are issued by banks, savings and loans, retail stores, and other businesses. Included are bank cards issued by banks and other financial institutions, prestige cards providing a high limit of credit and other benefits, affinity cards issued to groups of individuals with a common bond or tie, retail credit cards accepted only by the issuing retail establishment, and travel and entertainment cards that typically require payment of the entire balance when billed. Provided balances are paid in full as billed, they offer an attractive way of making purchases (and taking advantage of the float between time of purchase and time of payment). When balances are not paid in full, high rates of interest are charged. In 2004, the annual average finance rate charged by credit card plans was 14.7%.

A recent study done by a major credit bureau shows U.S. consumers are relying on their credit cards more than ever. According to Experian's latest National Score Index, compiled from a random sampling of three million consumers in the credit bureau's database, 51% of the U.S. population has at least two credit cards and 14% have 10 or more cards. Also, 14% are using at least half of their available credit, according to the same study. In 2001, over 44% of all United States families carried a balance on their credit card with a median debt of $1,900.

In contrast, a charge card is also used for making payments, but charges must be paid in full when the statement is received.

Debit Cards

The debit card may resemble a credit card in appearance, but functions more like a checking account. When a purchase is made, the transaction is immediately deducted from the cardholder's checking account. Because the debit card is machine-readable, funds can generally be withdrawn using ATMs. Unlike the credit card, a debit card does not have any float.

ELECTRONIC FUNDS TRANSFER (EFT)

Also referred to as the electronic funds transfer system (EFTS), this is the transfer of funds electronically rather than by check or cash. Application of this technology to consumer transactions includes ATMs found in banks and other convenient locations, Point of Sale Terminals (POS) used in retail establishments, preauthorized payments of mortgages and other recurring bills, automatic deposits of employee paychecks, telephone transfer systems, and Internet banking services.

Chapter 3

THE SCOPE OF FINANCIAL PLANNING

There is no universally recognized definition of financial planning. However, before discussing the financial planning process, it may be helpful to identify some of the activities and individuals that are commonly understood to be a part of the process. For instance, each of the following might reasonably stake a claim within the realm of "financial planning".

SINGLE TRANSACTION

From the perspective of the individual client, financial planning could mean nothing more than locating the least expensive credit card, or finding the best way to save for a child's college education. From the perspective of "financial planner," it could be the advice given by an investment adviser or stockbroker on what stocks the client should purchase, or the ledgers provided by a life insurance agent comparing the relative advantages and disadvantages of purchasing term or permanent life insurance. The difficulty here is that the process tends to be focused on doing, but is short on planning.

SOURCE AND DEPTH OF ADVICE

It could also be argued that financial planning does not begin until the individual client consults with his investment adviser, insurance agent, tax attorney, CPA, or other such advisor, on more in-depth matters relating to investment, insurance, or tax planning. Again, the difficulty here is that the process may be appropriately in-depth, but is narrow in scope and fails to consider all aspects of the client's financial situation.

COMPREHENSIVE PLANNING

And finally, there is the comprehensive must-do-it-all approach to financial planning. Clearly, this approach takes the high ground in maintaining that true financial planning involves a coordinated process of gathering facts relating to all areas of the client's financial affairs, determining the client's overall financial goals and objectives, and designing and implementing plans and strategies for attaining these goals. Although individuals involved in the financial planning process come from diverse backgrounds, the focus should not be so much on who is working with the client, but rather on assuring that the client receives comprehensive and in-depth advice that is implemented in coordination with the client's overall financial situation.

Another approach to defining "financial planning" might be to ask what the client should reasonably expect of persons holding themselves out as financial planners. If the process involves a fee for services, then clearly "comprehensive" financial planning is indicated.

But for many persons, the need for sound advice regarding specific investment, insurance, or tax planning issues clearly falls within the scope of financial planning.

WHY FINANCIAL PLANNING?

Only 42% of Americans know how much money to save for retirement.*

2005 Retirement confidence survey EBRI

During our lifetime we are constantly in the process of making, managing, banking, investing, protecting, and spending money. More often than not, we carry on intuitively from day to day, without taking the time to either plan or coordinate our financial affairs. Financial issues, problems, and decisions are compartmentalized. Many people, who would not dream of beginning a cross country road trip without a good road atlas, never even consider the importance of having a "financial road map" during the many years they will engage in earning and spending money. Without an adequate map, they are unlikely to reach a destination of financial freedom. The financial planning process should produce such a financial road map.

Today's decision to spend an extra $500 to upgrade to the promenade deck on a Caribbean cruise, or to spend an extra $6.95 per month for cable TV's super upgrade package, are typically made with little regard for the long-term impact on our financial future.

40% of retirees could be forced back into the workforce in the next 10 years because they didn't save enough for retirement.*

*Newstream.com 2004

In fact, each and every one of our day-to-day "spend or save" decisions will have a direct and calculable impact upon our financial well being in the years to come. Over a lifetime of making and spending money, the cumulative effect of these seemingly small decisions can be enormous. However, the degree of impact depends upon our individual time horizon, as demonstrated in the following table.

Small Decisions - Big Consequences

If Invested – Value of Funds

	10 yrs	20 yrs	30 yrs	40 yrs
$500 cruise upgrade	$1,041	$3,456	$8,670	$19,927
$6.95/month super TV package	$1,208	$3,816	$9,447	$21,605

Assumptions: funds are invested at 8% net after taxes, compounded annually.

Of course, the aforementioned is a very simplified example, but it makes the point. The financial planning process is important, not only in creating a "financial road map," but also in creating a better awareness of the short- and long-term consequences of every-day financial and consumption decisions. Once armed with this knowledge, financial planning will become a day-to-day exercise, not just a once-every-few-years or once-in-a-lifetime event.

THE FINANCIAL PLANNING PROCESS

The process of comprehensive financial planning is generally recognized to include the following seven steps:

Preliminary Meeting and Evaluation

During the initial interview, the financial planner and the prospective client get to know one another. This generally involves a first meeting during which the planner explains the nature of the services to be provided and the way in which he or she is paid for these services. In turn, the prospective client has an opportunity to determine whether the planner has the ability to offer the types of services that are needed.

The planner should take this opportunity to get some general idea of the prospective client's current financial position and long-term goals. It is important for both parties that the relationship begins on a basis of mutual trust and confidence.

If both parties decide to proceed, then the planner should provide the prospective client with an engagement letter that serves as a contract setting for the services to be provided, the charges for these services, and the client's responsibilities during the financial planning process.

If the planner is a registered investment advisor with the Securities and Exchange Commission (SEC), the planner will provide the prospective client with a "disclosure brochure" describing the services offered and the method by which the financial planner is compensated. SEC Rule 204-3 requires this disclosure.

Gather Information and Establish Goals

Effective planning cannot be done without gathering a substantial amount of information about the client. The information gathered can be either quantitative (e.g., financial information about the client's income, expenditures and assets) or qualitative (e.g., non-financial information about the client's risk tolerance, expectations about future standards of living, and health of the client and family members). Both the short-term and long-term goals of the client must be identified. Such a goal might be to have "adequate income in retirement," or to "provide for a child's education."

80% of your retirement income will be up to you.*

*Income of the Aged Chart book, Social Security Administration, 2004

In contrast to goals, at least one commentator uses the term "objectives" to indicate the shorter intermediate steps that must be accomplished in order to meet a goal. For example, in order to meet the goal of having adequate income in a retirement fund, an individual might establish the objective of setting aside 5% of net income in a retirement plan.

Goals must be both realistic and well defined. While "information gathering" and "goal setting" could be viewed as separate and distinct steps within the financial planning process, in truth, they are probably more effectively accomplished during the "give and take" of an interactive discussion between financial planner and client.

Once goals have been determined, it is essential to prioritize or rank them in order of importance. Some of the key financial and legal documents that must be secured during the data-gathering phase include:

1. **Wills, Trusts, and Powers of Attorney**
2. **Personal financial statements**
3. **Budgets**
4. **Retirement plan statements and brokerage and fund statements**
5. **Insurance policies (life, disability, health, property and casualty)**
6. **Divorce settlements**
7. **Federal and state income tax returns**
8. **Buy-sell agreements**

Analyze Information and Develop Plan

It is here that the planner takes the information obtained and agreed-upon client goals and translates them into a specific financial plan intended to achieve these goals using selected financial strategies and instruments. In effect, the plan translates client goals into specific actions steps. To assist in the process, the planner will often use computer programs to supplement a written analysis and recommendations. At a minimum, a comprehensive analysis generally includes a review of assets, liabilities, current and projected income, insurance coverage, and investment. Legal documents will also be examined and, if authorized by the client, the planner may seek the assistance of other professionals.

Present Plan

In presenting the plan, the financial planner meets with the client, explains the recommendations and provides the client with a copy of the written plan. However, before the formal plan presentation, the financial planner is well advised to informally discuss tentative observations and preliminary recommendations.

Such a discussion gives the planner an opportunity to address additional questions and items that arose during the design process, such as unrealistic client expectations and incomplete data. It is also an excellent means of allowing the client to participate in the design process and get client acceptance of key recommendations.

Without such client "buy in," it's unlikely that the final plan will be implemented, and that's what is most important. I personally believe, "A vision without implementation is a hallucination."

If necessary, the plan can then be revised prior to final presentation. The key elements of a written financial plan are likely to include the following:

1. Review of the client's stated goals
2. Analysis of the client's current situation, including both quantitative and qualitative data
3. Specific recommendations, to include actions, strategies and financial product recommendations
4. Action plan designed to implement the financial plan, to include time frames and assignment of responsibilities to named individuals

REMEMBER: A VISION WITHOUT IMPLEMENTATION IS A HALLUCINATION

Implement Plan

This stage is probably the most important of all. Plan implementation involves motivating the client to take the steps set forth in number 4 above. Typically, this may involve a variety of tasks, including the purchase and sale of investments, modification of insurance coverage, adoption of legal instruments and changes in spending and savings habits.

The plan may also include working with other professionals (e.g., check with the attorney that the new will and trust have not only been drafted and presented to the client, but that the client has signed them). Without implementation, the best of recommendations will fail and the client's objectives will not be reached.

Monitor Performance

Few, if any, financial plans are perfect and all clients are subject to changing circumstances. This stage involves evaluating the effectiveness of the plan in achieving the client's objectives. Unsatisfactory progress or performance requires that corrective action be taken (e.g., the market is down, the client becomes less risk tolerant, and the client is willing to accept lower returns and a reduced retirement lifestyle).

Periodically Review and Revise

Financial planning is not a goal, but rather an ongoing process. The client's personal circumstances will change and the financial plan must be adjusted accordingly. This may sound like I'm saying the same thing as in the previous paragraph, and I guess you could be right. But, so many times an investor will forget the periodic review and next thing you know three years later they find to their surprise that their 401-k has become a 201-k as a result of losses. Examples of reasons to conduct periodic reviews include: the client gets married or divorced, has a new child, experiences a change in health, changes jobs, suffers a financial setback, or experiences a financial windfall. Outside factors, such as changes in tax laws or the investment climate, must also be considered.

During periodic reviews, the assumptions underlying the original plan are evaluated and changes might be required. The review process presents an opportunity to identify these changes, update client information, and determine new or revised client goals. From here, the process and steps repeat themselves.

A final note about reviews – after you have gone through the process of selecting your advisor and developing a relationship, it is normal to achieve a level of comfort and trust. After all, the planner is managing your money and you need someone in this role whom you trust. However, do not allow this level of trust to prevent you from fulfilling your responsibilities as outlined earlier in this book. Please remember—you do not get what you expect, but you always get what you inspect!

Attain Goals

This is the "come and get it day." The client has sufficient funds to send his child to college, buy that second home, retire in the desired lifestyle at the intended time, or give a substantial offering at the end of the year to fund the spread of the gospel. Financial planning has played a very important part in achieving each of these goals.

> Finishing is better than starting.
> Ecclesiastes 7:8a (NLT)

TYPICAL GOALS OF FINANCIAL PLANNING

It has been said that financial planning involves risk management: For example, the risks of dying too soon, becoming disabled, or living too long. While this is certainly true, some of the following goals clearly fall outside of the concept of risk management, yet are important elements in many financial plans.

1. Improve current standard of living
2. Protect property from loss and damage
3. Protect family from large medical expenses
4. Reduce or eliminate debt, particularly high-interest credit card debt
5. Provide for ongoing income in case of disability
6. Create a reserve fund
7. Increase net worth through savings and investments
8. Minimize income taxes
9. Accumulate funds for specific large investments, such as weddings, vacations, homes, and extensive travels
10. Provide funds for child's education
11. Provide for a comfortable retirement
12. Protect family in case of client's premature death
13. Create an estate plan for disposition of assets at death
14. Pass business interest to surviving family members
15. Give funding annually for world-wide evangelism and missions
16. Tithe at death

THE FINANCIAL PLANNING DATA SHEET

A variety of forms are available to the financial planner, from the 10-minute drill to the 100-page compendium. Although it is generally agreed that it is better to have more rather than less information, the planner must be careful not to intimidate his client, particularly in the early stages of the financial planning process. So if you find yourself feeling intimidated, just ask the planner to provide you with a shorter version. On the other hand, an abbreviated form will likely yield insufficient information to develop a relevant and effective financial plan. The key with the data sheet is to strike a balance that is comfortable, but yet not insufficient where the planner is not able to adequately provide you with a plan. Remember—a false balance, the Bible informs us, is an abomination to the Lord, but a just weight is his delight. **(Proverbs 11:1; 20:23)**

Chapter 4

WHEN DO YOU NEED A PROFESSIONAL?

Often a specific event or need will trigger the desire for professional financial guidance. These might include:

> Ask, and it shall be given you; seek, and ye shall find; knock, and it shall be opened unto you
>
> Matthew 7:7

- **How to get out of debt God's Way**
- **Saving enough for retirement, or rolling over a pension or IRA**
- **Handling the inheritance of a large sum of money or other unexpected financial windfall**
- **Preparing for a marriage or a divorce**
- **Planning for the birth or adoption of a child**
- **Facing a financial hurdle, such as a serious illness, layoff or natural disaster**
- **Caring for aging parents or a disabled child**
- **Coping financially with the death of a spouse or close family member**
- **Funding education**
- **Buying, selling or passing on a family business**
- **Charitable giving**

Please keep in mind, Christians don't believe or confess some of the above barriers, such as divorce or serious illness, etc. However, you, or someone you know, may be faced with such challenges.

So, you should know how to handle whatever is thrown your way. Remember the Bible tells us that **"My people are destroyed for lack of knowledge." (Hosea 4:6).**

The very first thing I suggest you do is live a life of prayer and confess the blessings of God over you and your family each and every day. As Christians, we do this where healing is concerned. We even call it taking God's medicine. I suggest the very same principles for healing be applied to our finances. I call it **"Financial Vitamins."** Take or read financial Scriptures at least three times a day. Then seek out Godly counsel to steer you in the right direction or put you back on track.

DO YOU NEED THE SERVICES OF A FINANCIAL PROFESSIONAL?

How do you know if you could benefit from the services of a qualified Christian financial professional? If you do not have the time or the desire to actively plan and manage certain financial aspects of your life or you need help getting started, then you may benefit from an objective, third-party perspective on what are often emotional, difficult decisions.

In today's hectic world, it can be beneficial just to have a financial professional looking over your shoulder to double-check your efforts, to make sure you stay focused, and to follow through with your financial plans.

A CHRISTIAN FINANCIAL PROFESIONAL CAN HELP YOU:

- Understand what the Bible says about managing money. There are over 2,300 Scriptures in the Bible that speak about money. I believe this settles the fact that God has a plan for our finances, don't you?
- Set realistic family, financial and personal goals.
- Assess your current financial health by examining your assets, liabilities, income, insurance, taxes, investments and estate plans.
- Develop a realistic, comprehensive plan to meet your financial goals by addressing financial weaknesses and building on financial strengths, while applying faith.
- Put your plan into action and review its progress annually. Remember: **"But wilt thou know, O vain man, that faith without works is dead?" (James 2:20).**

The Way of the Christian

Choosing a financial professional is as important as choosing a doctor or lawyer. Working with a financial professional is a very personal relationship. In addition to competency, a financial professional should have integrity, trust, a commitment to ethical behavior and high professional standards.

You want a professional who will put your needs and interests first. Furthermore, as Christians, we should do our very best to seek out the help of a Christian financial professional based on the wisdom of God found in **Psalm 1:1-3.**

Many professionals specialize in working with certain types of clients, such as churches, pastors and their leaders, small-business owners, executives or retirees. Many have minimum income and asset requirements. Some specialize in certain areas of planning, such as retirement, estate planning, elder care or asset management. This is why I recommend that you interview the prospective professional to find the right one to serve your needs.

Before you engage an investment professional, make sure you know more about the investment professional than just their name and professional designation. The next chapter discusses some steps you can take to find an investment professional who can help you meet your financial goals.

> "...But seek ye first the Kingdom of God and his righteousness; and all these things shall be added unto you."
> Matthew 6:33

> My suggestion is that you find the wisest man in Egypt and put him in charge of a nationwide program. Let Pharaoh appoint officials over the land, and let them collect one-fifth of all crops during the seven good years. Have them gather all the grain of these good years into royal storehouses and store it away so there will be food in the cities.
>
> Genesis 41:33-36 (NLT)

Chapter 5

9 STEPS A CHRISTIAN SHOULD TAKE WHEN SELECTING A CHRISTIAN FINANCIAL PROFESSIONAL

1. Eliminate anxiety. This is done by praying first. If you are married, you and your spouse should pray together. By doing this you are seeking the Kingdom of God or God's ways of doing things, and He will give you guidance, which eliminates the anxiety that arises based on where you are versus where you think you should be. A biblical instruction on this is found in **Matthew 6:25-33.**

2. Think about your financial objectives and identify what type of financial services you need. There is a wide variation in the range of products and services that investment professionals offer. For example, some professionals can provide financial statement preparation and analysis. Others specialize in certain areas, such as taxes, estate planning, retirement planning, elder care, education, or risk management services.

In addition, some professionals may only be able to recommend a limited number of investment products. Knowing what you need will not only help you find the professional that's right for you, but will also prevent you from paying for services you don't need or want.

3. Get names of professionals from your pastor, church members, co-workers, neighbors, family or business associates. If you receive a name of an investment professional from an individual or group that you don't know, be certain to ask for several references. As a Christian, you should seek Godly advice, so find a professional who is laboring in the Word of God, as well as staying on the cutting edge of the financial service industry.

4. Talk with several professionals. Meet them face-to-face in their offices, if possible. Ask each of them about their professional background, education and Christian experience. Below are examples of the types of topics to discuss:
   - **Areas of specialization**
   - **Professional designations**
   - **Professional affiliations**
   - **Registrations or licenses**
   - **Education**
   - **Work history**
   - **Investment experience**
   - **Products and services**
   - **Types of clients the professional serves, and any minimum net worth or income requirements**
   - **How the professional prepares a plan**
   - **How the professional might address your particular needs**

EL ELYON- GOD MOST HIGH

This is the name which describes God as the SUPREME DEITY. "EL" denotes God as "the Strong One, first and only cause of things" and emphasizes the essence of the Godhead. "Elyon" describes God as "the Highest, the Exalted, the Supreme God." He is in the Highest place guarding and ruling over all things, making everything work to fulfill His divine plan and purpose. Abram had a revelation which brought him into a new relationship with "El Elyon." THE POWERFUL GOD, SUPREME GOD ABOVE ALL OTHER GODS…THE SUPREME GOD. As an act of worship, Abram gave El Elyon his tithe, a tenth of the spoils of the great victory God had given him over his enemies. Our privilege today is to give "El Elyon – God Most High" the highest place and highest priority in every area of our lives, including our giving and financial matters.

- Whether the professional or others will implement recommendations from the plan
- Business relationships the professional has that might present a conflict of interest
- Disciplinary history
- Whether the professional is a born-again, Spirit-filled believer (John 14:15-17)
- Whether the professional attends church regularly
- Whether the professional supports his local church with Tithes & Offerings (Malachi 3:8-11). As believers we should understand that giving always results in receiving from God (2 Cor. 9:6-7 and Luke 6:38). Further, if any individual is not a giver to the things of God, he will not be trusted with true riches (Luke 16:11). Thus, a financial professional who does not tithe would not be able to provide the best guidance to those who believe in God's Word and His promises.

5. Understand how you will pay for services. Investment professionals are typically paid in one or more of the following ways:

   - Hourly fee
   - Flat fee
   - Commission on the investment products they sell you
   - Percentage of the value of the assets they manage for you
   - Combination of fees and commissions

   Make sure you understand how the professional is compensated. The last thing you want is a financial adviser who has no money. Imagine having a dentist with no teeth, or a tailor with only one suit to his name. That would be **CRAZY!** Therefore, don't be cheap or look for something for nothing, because what you pay for is what you get—there is no free lunch. But, you shouldn't pay too much for advice either.

   Once you find a good fit, settle in your heart to properly compensate your financial professional. Remember your financial professional is a gift from God to edify the Body of Christ for the perfection of the saints. This way, he/she will not have to supplement his/her income by getting a second job or worry how to pay his/her bills.

   Think about it! If your financial professional has to get a second job, when will there be time to study the Word or stay on the cutting edge of the financial industry? The answer is, there won't be! You may want to review these Scriptures to understand where I'm coming from: **1 Timothy 5:17-18** and **Galatians 6:6.**

6. Ask whether he/she receives any additional compensation or financial incentives based on the products he/she sells. Sometimes investment professionals and their firms receive additional compensation for selling a particular product for one company compared to selling the same product for a different company.

7. Make sure that the investment professional and their firm are properly registered with the Financial Industry Regulatory Authority (FINRA), formerly known as NASD, the U.S. Securities and Exchange Commission, or a state insurance or securities regulator. Also learn about their professional background, business practices, and disciplinary history. Most investment professionals need to register as an investment adviser, investment advisory representative or broker/registered representative. Others may only be licensed to sell insurance. The FINRA Web site can be found on the Internet at www.NASD.com and can help you find registration and other background information on financial professionals.

8. Check out any professional designation by contacting the issuing organization and determining whether the financial planner is currently authorized to use the designation and whether he/she has been disciplined.

   Make sure you understand the requirements for a professional designation. The criteria used by the organizations that grant professional designations for investment professionals vary greatly. Some require formal certification procedures, including examinations and continuing professional education credits. Others may merely signify that membership dues have been paid.

9. If the investment professional will sell you investment products, ask if the firm they work for is a member of the Securities Investor Protection Corporation (SIPC). SIPC provides limited customer protection if a firm becomes insolvent. Also ask if the firm has other insurance that provides coverage beyond the SIPC limit. SIPC does not insure against losses attributable to a decline in the market value of your securities, only against insolvency.

Remember, the most important part of making the right investment decision is seeking the Lord first (**Matthew 6:33).**

Follow these nine steps and you will find the investment professional that best meets your financial needs. Do not rush. Do your background investigation. Resist investment professionals that urge you to immediately hire them, and avoid working with individuals who aren't born-again, Spirit-filled Christians.

Only 42 percent of U.S. workers have tried to determine how much they will need to save for a comfortable retirement.[1]

1. Employee Benefit Research Institute, 2005

How much retirement income will you need? Should you refinance your mortgage? How much life insurance is enough? What type of IRA is right for you?

Our financial calculators are designed as educational tools to help you estimate answers to common financial questions. They are not intended to predict future returns or results. Simply go to our website at www.ncfallc.com and click on one of the general financial topics. You'll find a selection of easy-to-use calculators about related financial topics.

Chapter 6

FULL DISLOSURE

The Lord hates cheating, but he delights in honesty Proverbs 11:1 (NLT)	Good people are guided by their honesty; treacherous people are destroyed by their dishonesty Proverbs 11:3 (NLT)

At the heart of any working relationship is honesty and trust. A relationship with a financial professional is no different. Trust is built on two factors: First, knowing that the professional is acting in your best interest; and second, full disclosure of the professional's background, business practices and other issues.

Full disclosure means the professional is forthright in providing answers about his/her Christian walk, background, experience, and business methods. Chapter 5 provides a list of topics to explore. I encourage you to raise these topics and to be concerned if you think the professional is not forthcoming with information.

The financial professional should also disclose any disciplinary actions that may have been taken against him/her by government regulatory agencies or clients. You can confirm whether a disciplinary action has been taken against a particular registered representative by visiting the FINRA Web site at www.NASD.com.

If you do not receive full disclosure from a financial professional, it is a good indicator you should take your financial needs elsewhere.

DON'T BE DUPED!

Remember to inquire about a financial professional's credentials. Financial analyst, financial adviser, financial consultant, financial professional, investment consultant, and wealth manager all are generic terms or job titles used to refer to investment professionals. Anyone can use these terms without registering with securities regulators or meeting any educational and experience requirements. Occasionally, I run across individuals who say they are financial professionals only to find out they are not; yet they advise Christians and people in general regarding their money. Some have even gone so far as to write books. So be mindful, and **DON'T BE DUPED!**

...WITH ALL THY GETTING GET UNDERSTANDING

Proverbs 4:7

Investors can sometimes become confused by the many designations used by investment professionals. I should know. I have five. You should ask the professional about such designations then follow up with the granting organization to better understand what education and experience requirements are necessary for a designation and whether the granting organization mandates continuing education.

You should also determine if there is a public disciplinary process, a means to check a professional's status, and otherwise ensure that a professional designation is more than just a string of letters behind his name.

Another helpful hint is to know that the **FINRA/NASD Rule of Conduct 2210** prohibits brokerage firms and brokers registered with FINRA/NASD from referencing nonexistent or self-conferred degrees or designations or referencing legitimate degrees or designations in a misleading manner.

Chapter 7

INTEGRITY: THE KEY TO A SUCCESSFUL CLIENT AND ADVISER RELATIONSHIP

> The just man walketh in his integrity; his children are blessed after him
> Proverbs 20:7

All Christians should operate in honesty and integrity. In fact, they should treat their neighbors as they would themselves. I don't know anybody who would cheat, lie or defraud himself. Unfortunately, however, we know that not all Christians operate in such a way. Non-believers may be even less likely to operate in this manner since they don't purpose to live by the higher standard of God's Word.

Below you will find the professional code of ethics adopted by the financial professionals associated with our firm, National Christian Financial Advisors, Inc. (NCFA):

- As a Christian financial professional, I will continue to put God first and serve Him until the coming of our Lord and Savior Jesus Christ.

- I will continue to study the word of God to show myself approved unto God, a workman that needeth not to be ashamed, rightly dividing the word of truth. **2 Timothy 2:15.**

- I will do my part to share the good news of our Lord and Savior Jesus Christ, which also includes supporting my local church with tithes & offerings.

- As a professional, I will place the interests of my clients first.

- I will continually seek to maintain and improve my professional knowledge, skills and competence.

- I will obey applicable laws and regulations and avoid any conduct or activity which would cause unjust harm to those who rely upon my professional judgment and skill.

- I will be diligent in the performance of all my occupational duties.

- I will help improve public trust and confidence in the securities industry by being an example of integrity and by adopting such Code of Ethics.

Chapter 8

KNOW YOUR RIGHTS AND RESPONSIBILITIES AS AN INVESTOR

YOUR RIGHTS AS AN INVESTOR

Investors have a right to professionalism and a high standard of performance from their financial professionals. The following "checklist" offers guidelines for the Christian Financial Professional's level of commitment to his/her walk as a believer and the service you should expect to receive.

- ✓ Born-again Spirit Filled Believer
- ✓ Supports local church in tithes & offerings
- ✓ Attends church on a regular basis
- ✓ Operates the practice with honesty, integrity and excellence
- ✓ Provides competent, courteous, and timely service
- ✓ Confidentially treats all personal information
- ✓ Makes investment recommendations that are based upon your needs and objectives, and consistent with your financial goals
- ✓ Offers clear explanations of all recommendations, including the potential risks and benefits of investments
- ✓ Executes transactions in a timely manner
- ✓ Provides accurate, user-friendly account statements
- ✓ Responds promptly to any issues or complaints
- ✓ Provides information on industry experience and expertise upon request

YOUR RESPONSIBILITIES AS AN INVESTOR

In order for any relationship to be fruitful and productive, both parties have to live up to their end. Otherwise you run the risk of failure or burn out. Fulfill your part and position yourself to receive the best advice available. Below are a few things for which you, the investor, are responsible:

- Provide complete information to your financial professional about your income, net worth, tax status, investment experience, age and occupation, tithing, investment objectives and risk tolerance. Be open and clear about your current financial situation and goals, and contact your financial professional if there are any changes in your situation or circumstances. Remember that this person is equipped spiritually and professionally to be a blessing to you and he/she is a gift from God and, therefore, anointed to help you. Without knowing your situation, your professional is not able to best serve you.
- Be prayerful about your financial situation from start to finish. The Bible tells us that we should pray without ceasing **(1 Thessalonians 5:17).** You should be praying and uplifting your financial professional so he/she continues in faith, operates under the anointing of God and handles all his/her affairs in honesty and integrity **(Hebrews 13:18).**
- Always consult an attorney or an accountant for specific legal or tax advice. Your questions can best be answered by a qualified professional with expertise in a specified field.
- Assume decision-making responsibility for your accounts. Evaluate the advice of your financial professional and determine which actions to take.

Also, educate yourself in the basics of financial markets, the nature of risk and other aspects of investing. You should be able to make reasoned judgment about investment recommendations. It is also your responsibility to make the decisions regarding purchases and sales of securities within your accounts.

- Request and read prospectuses and other applicable material carefully before making any purchases. It is important that you have a clear understanding of the potential risks and benefits of any investment. If you have any questions about the information, ask your financial professional.
- Review all statements and confirmations, and immediately report any errors to your financial professional. Your financial professional should be able to quickly provide you with answers to such questions.
- Have cash or securities available in your account at the time of a transaction. The Securities and Exchange Commission (SEC) requires payment for purchases by settlement date (three business days after the purchase).
- Never make any payments for securities payable to a financial professional or to an entity controlled by a financial professional, nor any individual or entity that is not registered within your resident state, the SEC or FINRA (formerly known as NASD) as a broker-dealer.
- Do not loan any money or securities to, or borrow them from, a financial professional. Specifically, do not authorize or permit a financial professional to act as personal custodian of your securities, stock powers, money or any other personal or real property which you own.

Chapter 9

Every investor should know the **ELEVEN BASIC KEYS FOR BETTER INVESTING:**

> Wisdom is the principal thing; therefore get wisdom; and with all thy getting get understanding
>
> Proverbs 4:7

1. If an investment seems too good to be true, it probably is. The first rule of investing is this: Higher investment returns are always accompanied by higher risks.

2. It is generally recommended that you diversify over a broad spectrum of investments. Your financial professional can help you select asset classes which are appropriate for you.

3. Be patient. Stick to your plan. Employ a dollar cost averaging strategy and approach to the market with a long-term point of view.

4. Don't succumb to fear when the market is dropping and don't become greedy when prices are rising.

5. Emotions can be the greatest enemy to your long-term investment plan. History has shown that when most investors are selling, you may have been better off buying.

6. Stay in touch with your financial professional. Be honest about your concerns. Ask questions, especially about risks or sales charges.

7. Approach investing like you would any important goal – get involved in the process.

8. Always read the prospectus. Do your best to understand the risks, costs and liquidity of any investment you make. If there are sections of the prospectus you don't understand, ask your financial professional to explain.

9. Design an investment plan suited to your individual circumstances. Monitor your results and make adjustments if necessary to keep on track. Your financial professional has the tools and skills to guide you through the financial planning process.

10. Gain understanding of your starting point. What are your resources; your risk tolerance; your time horizon; your goals and objectives?

11. Consider strategic asset allocation – a sophisticated, long-term approach to investing. Strategic asset allocation provides the blueprint, which helps you diversify your assets into the appropriate asset classes with proper balance. However, it doesn't prevent loss.

Chapter 10

COUNT THE COST BEFORE INVESTING

> For which of you, intending to build a tower, sitteth not down first, and counteth the cost, whether he have sufficient to finish it?
> Luke 14:28

There are two ways in which a financial professional may be established: **(1) as a salaried employee of a firm, or (2) as an independent contractor, which means he/she is not employed, and is not paid a salary by any firm.** Instead, that individual earns commissions or fees based on the activity in their clients' accounts and/or assets in their portfolios. Generally, commissions range from 1% to 7% of the principal amount of the trade and are disclosed in writing either in the prospectus or the sales confirmation.

Some firms offer asset management programs as an alternative to the commission structure. In this type of program, you are not charged commissions for purchases or sales of securities in your account.

Instead, your account is charged a quarterly advisory fee. Annual advisory fees generally range from .75% to 2.35%. For some accounts, there may also be a transaction charge ranging from $10 to $40.

Stocks and Bonds

Generally, the purchase or sale of stocks and bonds is executed on an agency basis (that is, the firm acts as an "agent" on your behalf to conduct the transaction). Stock and bond commissions typically range from 1% to 5%, depending on the size of the trade and number of shares. The commission is added to the principal amount of a purchase or subtracted from the proceeds of a sale. Your financial professional may negotiate a **"discount"** on the commission in certain instances.

Mutual Funds

Mutual funds are classified either as **"load"** (meaning a commission is paid to the financial professional) or **"no load"** (meaning the services of a financial professional are not used and no commission is paid). Load funds can be further divided into many classes, or types. Some of the most common classes are described below. In addition to mutual fund commissions, the financial professional may also receive a service fee, known as a "12b-1 fee" (not all funds offer multi-class pricing, and not all funds have 12b-1 fees. These fees generally are 25/100 of 1% for equity funds and less for income funds). This fee is deducted from the net asset value (NAV) of your mutual fund and paid quarterly to your financial professional.

Here is how each class of share you purchase works:

"A" Shares

- Initial sales charge at time of purchase
- May offer volume (breakpoint) discounts
- Lower 12b-1 fees

"B" Shares

- No initial sales charge
- Sales charge is amortized over time
- Subject to a contingent deferred sales charge if the minimum investment period is not met, typically 7-8 years, sometimes shorter.
- Expenses will exceed those of "A" shares over time, which will impact long-term performance
- Breakpoints are usually not available

"C" Shares

- No initial sale charge
- May have a one year or longer contingency with a level low ongoing (amortized) sales charge.
- Generally higher 12b-1 fees
- Available for institutional and/or high initial investment clients
- Appropriate for investors with short investment horizons or who wish to "pay as they go"

Chapter 11

A QUICK WORD ON BUDGETS

Bud-get: **a:** *A statement of the financial position of an administration for a definite period of time based on estimates of expenditures during the period and proposals for financing them; b: a plan for the coordination of resources and expenditures; c: the amount of money that is available for, required for, or assigned to a particular purpose. (Merriam-Webster's Dictionary)*

Getting out of debt and maintaining your lifestyle over the long term can be challenging. Without following God's financial system and a reasonable budgeting plan, it is difficult to effectively manage spending. To help you evaluate how well you are balancing your income vs. your expenses and determine your net cash flow, please visit our website at www.NCFALLC.com and use the cash flow analysis form. In the meantime, here is a quick word on "Budgets."

In certain Christian circles, the word budget is sacreligious or seen as not operating in faith. This is completely incorrect and can not be substantiated by the word of God. This point of view is akin to saying wearing glasses is not of faith or taking glycerin for your heart is not of faith because you are believing God for healing.

None of these statements is correct because wearing glasses never healed anybody's eyes, nor has taking glycerin healed a person's heart. They simply allow you to function normally while you wait for your healing to occur.

If a person believed in such statements, they would actually be putting their faith in the glasses, glycerin or a budget instead of God.

Putting a budget together will help you effectively manage your finances and keep you on course as you strive to achieve your stated goals and objectives. In fact, God's word is quite clear about budgeting, accounting and maintaining order.

For which of you, intending to build a tower, sitteth not down first, and counteth the cost, whether he have sufficient to finish it?

Luke 14:28

Let all things be done decently and in order.

1 Corinthians 14:40

It is difficult to manage a household successfully without a budget. It can be done, but there are often unintended negative consequences. An example of good accounting is seen in Matthew 25 in the parable of a master dealing with his servants to whom he gave talents.

After a long time the Lord of those servants cometh, and reckoneth with them.

Matthew 25:19

The word "reckoneth" is not even a theological term; it is an accounting term and one of its definitions is "to cast up or settle accounts".

Now ask yourself, how are you going to settle an account if you have no way of determining what you started with? You also will not be able to explain what you did with what you had.

So please don't be afraid or think you are not operating in faith by establishing a budget. Being a good financial steward is truly God's way. A budget will enable you to be faithful with little so God can give you authority over much. Conversely, don't use a budget to keep you from doing what the Lord is calling you to do by saying "we don't have enough."

> And he said unto him, Well done, thou good servant; because thou has been faithful in a very little, have thou authority over ten cities.
> Luke 19:17

Always remember that a false balance is an abomination to the Lord. Always start you budget in prayer, and if at the end you come up short, seek the Lord for guidance and direction before pursuing. If God has called you to do whatever you are setting out to do, all the money may not be there at the beginning. Don't worry; I personally have never had all the money in place when God has called me to do something, nor have I come up short when doing what God has called me to do.

Finally, a budget is like a guardrail for your finances, similar to a guardrail alongside the road. Without guardrails on the road, you could fall off a cliff. Likewise, without the financial guardrail of a budget, you are more than likely going to fall off the financial cliff of life and possibly cause financial ruin for you and your family.

Chapter 12

HELP! I TITHE BUT I'M STILL BROKE!

TITHES & OFFERINGS

It is impossible to write a Christian book, which is designed to improve your financial picture, without thoroughly discussing tithes & offerings. As Christians, this is the foundation for our financial success and freedom.

Every kingdom or government has a system in which their citizens are governed. In the United States, we have the Democratic or Constitutional Republic system and our commerce is based on capitalism or free trade. Some countries have a system based on communism and their commerce is socially driven. No matter how you look at it or what you think, every kingdom has a system and God calls His system "The Kingdom of God," which operates by "Seedtime and Harvest."

While the earth remaineth, "Seedtime and Harvest," and cold and heat, and summer and winter; and day and night shall not cease.

Genesis 8:22

The mere fact that you are reading this book lets you and I both know that the earth still remaineth.

Therefore, this established law and principle is still at work just like gravity, whether you know how it works or you disagree with it.

You say in your heart: "I don't have enough"! I say, **"You have sowed either little or nothing; therefore, you keep receiving little or nothing."** To change where you are, you must change your mind, your speech, who you believe, and ultimately, what you sow.

Be not deceived; God is not mocked; for whatsoever a man soweth, that shall he also reap.

Galatians 6:7

A PARADIGM SHIFT

Paradigm: *One of Merriam-Webster's definitions for paradigm is a philosophical and theoretical framework of a scientific school of discipline within which theories, laws, and generalizations and the experiments performed in support of them are formulated; broadly; a philosophical or theoretical framework of any kind.*

Every place I go, I am confronted with the same story: Slightly more than 20 percent of church members tithe. So I decided to research this figure in relationship to the financial standing of the church at large. The findings revealed some serious truths—truths that require, in my opinion as a Minister of the Gospel, a PARADIGM shift, first on the part of those of us who teach the Bible, then with believers who hear and really want to please the Father by living a victorious financial lifestyle based on God's word.

Another statement I hear frequently is how "blessed" people have been by their tithing. "Brother Hakeem", they say, "from the day I started tithing, God started blessing my finances."

With such passion I hear, "Our bills are all current, we are now able to take a nice vacation each year, and we have a modest savings and retirement plan that is growing, albeit, at about the same rate as inflation." Some even say they are out of debt with a pre-owned car and all the payments are current.

SILENT FRUSTRATION

On the flip side and more commonplace, once you get through the religion, I hear, "Brother Hakeem, we tithe, but it leaves us with very little, making us unable to meet our other financial obligations." This is probably the hardest to hear—the hurt and despair of God-fearing, Spirit-filled, tongue-talking Christians who are living in silent frustration. These people have nobody to share their frustrations with, for fear of being labeled as either a robber, under the curse, or lacking faith. They know there is a better way, but yet they are not experiencing all that Father God has for them.

This is not my first time encountering such statements and experiences. When I was a young boy going to church with my grandmother, I heard it. As a teenager attending church with my mother, however, my mother remained a faithful tither regardless of how poor we were. And now, as a minister of the gospel traveling around the country and abroad, I still see and hear it.

In fact, I have heard these very statements for over thirty years as an adult. If you factor in my youth, I've been hearing this for well over fifty years.

I believe this has come about as a result of misinterpreting the passage in **Malachi 3:10** that tells us to tithe and God will…**open you the windows of heaven, and pour you out a blessing, that there shall not be room enough to receive it.**

As a financial adviser, I always had trouble believing the best God had for me or the body of Christ was just being able to pay my bills on time, a little retirement money, and a house and a used car—but before even getting to that point, you may have to live paycheck-to-paycheck. The world offers far more without being a crook or cheating. In worldly terms, all you have to do is work hard and spend within your limits. So I knew God had to have better for me—and He does, but not too many people could show me how and even fewer were able to share that He did.

However, Sunday after Sunday, Wednesday after Wednesday, and yes, Friday after Friday, this is what is being taught and what is being experienced throughout churches all over the world. It was not until I asked God to give me a revelation from his word on finances and to enable me to use the gifts and talents He gave me to excel as a financial adviser that He began to show me.

A PARADIGM SHIFT is needed, especially when ten, twenty, thirty and even forty years later we have gone around this financial mountain in a modern type of wilderness experience. Don't get me wrong. I am not saying the teaching was done intentionally. On the contrary, I believe good God-fearing ministers and saints really want to do what is right, but they have not received a revelation of tithes and offerings, and how to appropriate the reciprocal blessings into their lives. They are merely products of what they were taught, so the vicious cycle continues.

Here are the findings according to the statistics and analysis from a national survey conducted by Barna Research:

Reported giving to the local church

- 9% of born again Christians tithed their income to churches in 2004.
- The average cumulative donations to churches by evangelicals totaled $2097. (2000) Among the born again population, which represents 38% of all adults, the average giving to churches in 2003 was $1411, much higher than a year earlier ($1220), but below previous year's totals. (2004)
- Close to two out of every three households (63%) donated some money to a church, synagogue or other place of religious worship during 2003. That percentage has remained constant since 2001, but is somewhat lower than the number of Church donors identified in 2000 and in 1999 (66%).
- When contributions are examined as a percentage of household income, giving to religious centers represents about 2.2% of gross income. (2003)
- In total, one out of every twenty households (5%) tithed their pre-tax income to non-profit organizations. (2003)

Groups that are Most and Least Likely to Give

- The segments that were most likely to give at least ten percent to their house of worship included evangelicals (14% did so); adults with an active faith (12% of those who had attended church, prayed and read the Bible during the previous week); African-Americans, born agains, charismatic or Pentecostal Christians, and people from households with a gross income of $60,000 or more (7% among each of those segments).
- The segments that were least likely to tithe included Catholics (1%) as well as non-born again individuals, adults under 35, and those from households with a gross income of $40,000 to $59,999 (2% of the people in each of those segments tithed). (2003)

Clearly you can see by these statistics that something is wrong with today's application of tithes and offerings. And if something is wrong with the application of faith in God's financial system, then I submit it's because of what is being taught. **Remember faith comes by hearing and hearing by the word of God…Romans 10:17.**

The other astonishing fact here is African-Americans are among the group most likely to give at least ten percent to their house of worship. As a collective people, however, they are one of the poorest people groups in the United States, and that is a complete contradiction of the word. You should never be in a position where you are giving but end up in lack. So something is wrong!

STEP 1 IN THE CHANGE PROCESS

The **first** PARADIGM SHIFT must be found within the five fold ministry that teaches God's people. The current view is to blame believers for not wanting to tithe and then say they are going to be cursed. In fact, however, true born again Spirit filled believers not only want to give, but have the essence of givers inside of them.

The Bible tells us that when you accept Jesus as your Lord and Savior, you are a new creature. Your spirit is renewed and your body becomes the temple of the Holy Ghost, and His nature is to be a giver.

Then what is the problem? The common thought is, "Their flesh, brother Hakeem. You see, their flesh is not renewed, while their Spirit is." I used to believe that until I started speaking with hundreds, if not thousands, of God's people and found out differently. Your flesh may apply to drinking or sexual sin. These sins are learned behaviors and/or deal with the flesh, but contrary to popular belief, the flesh doesn't pertain to giving.

Giving is a **NATURE,** and it is **SPIRITUAL**, and an act of **LOVE**, and **God Himself**, who is **LOVE**, demonstrates this nature and spiritual principle by giving His only begotten son.

For God so <u>loved</u> the world, that he gave his only begotten Son, that whosoever believeth in him should not perish, but have everlasting life.

John 3:16

Therefore, I submit it's not a flesh battle; it's a faith or trust battle. If a person tries something and doesn't get results, it is human nature to revert back to what you believe has worked.

If asked, most believers at some point in their Christian walk tithed and may have stopped, but found themselves, in their eyes, not benefiting from this new system. So again, it is not flesh, but a lack of faith or trust in God's financial system, based on their lack of knowledge, experience and revelation of tithes and offerings.

STEP 2 IN THE CHANGE PROCESS

The **Second** PARADIGM SHIFT must take place with the saints of God in the way they are interpreting the scriptures, especially **Malachi 3:10.** Most people refer to the **TITHE** to bring into the store house of God and the discussions are all based on the **tithe, robbing God and being cursed.** Rarely is anything ever mentioned about **offerings.**

I am convinced that these saints that I previously mentioned who say they are blessed are really not seeing the full effect of the plan of tithing on their income, but merely experiencing the benefits that good budgeting brings to a person who starts to tithe.

I have never met a tither who didn't have a budget, have you? Most, if not all, tithers I know operate on a budget of some sort, and anyone on a budget, including a lost drug dealer, can pay his/her bills if he/she is disciplined in spending by a budget.

Their **"financial blessings",** therefore, are not the result of spiritual law, but the result of the natural law of accounting.

The situation of those who are living paycheck-to-paycheck, not tithing, or tithing and barely making it is more than likely the result of little faith in God's financial system. Or, they are violating one of the practical principles of money management.

While faith is designed to bring them what they desire, they have not yet developed it and are not willing to wait, so they go ahead and get it by natural means by over-extending themselves. By understanding the simple principle of living within one's means, an individual will be able to keep himself from being broke.

We as ministers must start telling the truth...**And ye shall know the truth and the truth shall make you free—John 8:33.** The implication here is that the truth you know and act on will make you free; the truth by itself will not make you free. If that were the case, every sinner that goes into a motel to have sexual pleasure would get saved because there right next to them in the drawer is a Gideon Bible.

The other point I want to bring to your attention is that the reverse of this scripture is true as well. What truth you don't know will keep you in bondage, and the lack of truth about money has done just that for over two thousand years.

I meet literally thousands of Christians each year, and I have not met a Christian who has told me "Brother Hakeem, since I've been tithing, God has poured me out a blessing *I just can't contain.*"

In fact, I was in Georgia not too long ago for a minister's conference with about six thousand in attendance. Surely someone there would have had a testimony saying, "I can't find another bank that will take my money here in town. I currently have 10 bank accounts all with **$100,000** each in them and the local banks refuse to take my money. They tell me it's because they cannot insure it any longer with FDIC. They say to go down the block where the manager is waiting for you to come in to sign the account over to you. It has **$500,000**, in it. God bless you!"

Or, "Brother Hakeem I have too many houses, control too many fortune 500 hundred companies, own an airline, not just a jet, but an airline—here you take one."

Or, "You see "Brother Hakeem, I don't know if you know it or not, but the Bible is certainly right. If you tithe, God will pour out a blessing that just cannot be contained."

The truth is the people I am meeting truly love the Lord and they are tithers, but find themselves living paycheck-to-paycheck, and in most cases they are broke, with very few of us as the exceptions.

I am not going to dissect this chapter and verse for I believe others before me have done a great job explaining the italic verses and the fact that you must do more than give or return your tithe—you must also give offerings. I remind you that if you are only tithing, then you are not benefiting from God's financial system to the fullest. You are a member, but not reaping the complete benefits. However, I will point out two things from this chapter and verse, which I believe are from Heaven and where the PARADIGM SHIFT must take place.

Child of God, I want you to come to a totally new understanding about the tithe and offering. I desire to be used of God to help you obtain financial freedom that will take you beyond just an orderly execution of financial obligations each month and into a reality of true financial freedom. Such freedoms that will allow you to have exceedingly abundantly more than enough, so that you can be a blessing to others and help bring Salvation to all, which is one of the original Greek words for Rich. ***Ploutevw: means affluent in resources so that he can give blessings of Salvation to all.***

I pray you can receive this as well as see yourself in the position of wealth and having the ability to have your needs and wants met with plenty left over, while operating a great giving ministry and supplying resources to the ministries you so long to support. Let us begin with a new intensive look at the scripture you have probably read hundreds of times:

Will a man rob God? Yet ye have robbed me. But ye say, Wherein have we robbed Thee? In tithes and offerings. Ye are cursed with a curse for ye have robbed me, even this whole nation.

Malachi 3:8-9

I want to bring your attention to the very first verse, **"Will a man rob God?" And verse 9, "Ye are cursed with a curse…"** It is these two statements where I truly believe a PARADIGM SHIFT is needed in how it is being taught.

Please don't close the book thinking I am introducing heresy. The devil is probably talking to you right now, saying, "You see you can't trust financial advisors; he doesn't know what he's talking about. What man of God would dare say that?" Child of God, hear the voice of the Lord by the leading of the Spirit. God wants you to get this revelation into your spirit so you can receive all that Jesus paid for on the cross. If you have to stop and say a prayer to fight the thought bombs, do so! Do whatever you must to hear what the Spirit of God is saying.

Alright, it states **"Will a man rob God?"** This scripture and verse, in fact the entire book, is addressing a Nation who robbed God. Now, you first need to understand that they had experienced the blessing of tithing, giving and offerings, but they forgot and started living wrong, giving blemished and polluted offerings, and talking against God. Even the Priest was partaking in such activities.

You see Child of God, the entire book of Malachi, including the third chapter, was never intended to be a foundation for tithing or giving offerings. Perhaps this is why some have confused tithing as being Old Testament. This chapter was sent by God to His chosen people to rebuke them and bring forth correction through His messenger Malachi, giving them the opportunity to repent and start fresh. In other words, wipe the slate clean.

Yet in the Body of Christ, **Malachi 3:8-10** is used Sunday after Sunday to take an offering. Most people don't even read verse 11, which is extremely important to know. In fact, when you read verses 11 through 18, you get a picture of the true benefits of tithing and giving offerings, but you just cannot get that from verses 8 through 10.

Further, every time this scripture is read in church for an offering, **FAITH** is quenched instead of increased, especially if you are a person that tithes and gives offerings. This scripture doesn't even pertain to you because you are not robbing God. So I refer to this scripture as the **"robbers"** and should only be used to rebuke, correct and teach what will happen if you forget God, not as a scripture to build faith in God's financial system of continued supernatural provisions.

TITHING THE TITHE

The givers scripture is found in **Deuteronomy 26:1-15**. The tithe is the percentage, which is 1/10 or ten percent. That's the amount, but what you do is tithe the tithe.

Deuteronomy 26:1-15 gives a detailed description of what you should do with first fruit, tithes and offerings, known as tithing the tithe, which is an act.

This is the scripture that should be taught and read after an offering, starting from verse 13 through 15. If so, I firmly believe faith will come and the people of God will begin to walk in the fullness of God's financial system of tithes and offerings.

YOU ARE NOT CURSED!

Now for the second point I want to discuss. Malachi 3:9 states, **"Ye are cursed with a curse".** Again, I say we must teach the whole truth and nothing but the truth in order for God to endorse His word and for the listener to receive faith to begin activating what they are learning.

Every time I hear **"Ye are cursed with a curse,"** my heart cries out and wants to say, "**STOP**, you do not have to say that to receive an offering from God's people. If you want them to give just ask."

These verses bring rebuke, correction, and condemnation, causing people to give for a few weeks or maybe several months and then stop again. This craziness has been going on for almost forty years, if not more.

Let us look at the word of God to better understand where I am coming from. In the book of **Acts 10:1-3**, there was a man by the name of Cornelius, a centurion of the band called the Italian band. He was a devout man, yet not Spirit filled, and one that feared God with his entire house, which gave much alms to the people and prayed to God always. This devout man had an encounter with an angelic being because of his giving and prayers; God was moved and commissioned Peter to go witness to him so he may receive the Holy Ghost and be baptized.

Nevertheless, Peter, like many Pastors and ministers today, said during a visitation from God himself:

*...**Not so, Lord; for I have never eaten any thing that is common or unclean. And the voice spake unto him again the second time, what God hath cleansed, that call not thou common...***

Acts 10:14-15.

Peter was so entrenched in his religious teachings and customs that God Himself had to speak to Peter by way of vision, not once, but three times to give him instructions and to not call what he cleaned through the blood of Jesus, unclean and common. Yet Peter still doubted, like many Pastors and ministers today doubt. They teach that if you don't tithe, you're cursed. But God has said and continues to say ***"...What God hath cleansed, that call not thou common..." or cursed!***

By the grace of God Peter yielded, but was still doubtful as we see in verse 28. Peter had to let it be known what he felt and thought. While giving a long dissertation on the matter, the Spirit of God fell on Cornelius and all that were in his house. **(Verse 44)**

You see, unclean and common is just another way of saying cursed, yet we see Peter himself had to have a PARADIGM SHIFT.

Let's look at another verse of scripture demonstrating that ministers should not call God's people cursed. It is found in the book of Galatians.

Christ hath redeemed us from the curse of the law, being made a curse for us; for it is written, Cursed is every one that hangeth on a tree; that the blessing of Abraham might come on the Gentiles through Jesus Christ.

Galatians 3:13-14

Like an attorney presenting a case in front of a group of jurors, the evidence of the two scriptures I shared above must be presented. The Bible tells us: ***But if he will not hear thee, then take with thee one or two more, that in the mouth of two or three witnesses every word may by established. Matthew 18:16.*** Having read the evidence, the jury deliberates, conclusively returns to the courtroom, hands the verdict to the Judge (Jesus), and the Judge shakes his head and returns the verdict for reading.

The foreperson stands up and states, "Due to overwhelming evidence, we the jury conclusively decide that ***Malachi 3:9; "Ye are cursed with a curse..."*** is guilty and cast into the bottomless pit and sentenced to death and no longer able to be used as a tithe and offering scripture before God's people."

I don't know about you, but I can hear all of the accused saints and their loved ones before them crying out and shouting for **JOY**--free at last, free at last, Christ has redeemed us, we are free at last. Heaven and the entire host of angels are singing **PRAISES! WORTHY IS THE LAMB THAT WAS SLAIN…**

I pray this has been a blessing to you and has released the burden I know so many have carried for years. It is my deepest prayer that you receive this teaching and allow the provisions of Jehovah Jirah to meet and exceed your every need and want, that we may fulfill the promise given Abraham and fulfilled by Jesus, blessed to be a blessing.

Then the plan that God has for funding the church, television ministries and world evangelism through tithes and offerings will be accomplished by the faithful execution of His financial system of **"Seedtime and Harvest". And remember, Tithing should be an act of "LOVE" not a commandment!**

Before leaving this chapter, to ensure that you understand what to do if you are tithing and giving offerings, but yet find yourself broke, I want to give you a check list of some items that may be helpful in examining your situation. Maybe one of these items is the reason why you aren't receiving the blessings of financial increase. Please understand that this list is not exhaustive, but it is a list that my wife and I use when things appear to be out of sync.

In addition, after counseling and planning for thousands of people, I've concluded that the problems we all deal with center around either our soul (i.e., mind, will, intellect and emotions) or our body (i.e., how we treat it or not, whether unintentionally or intentionally). It could be argued to include Spirit too, since we are a tri-part creature based on 1 Thessalonians 5:23. But I would disagree because our spirit was dealt with by God the day we received Jesus Christ as our Lord and Savior, while the soul and body were left to us to continuously change and renew according to Romans 12:1-2 and 1 Corinthians 9:27.

SPIRITUAL CHECKLIST

1. Tither: One who continues to tithe until Jesus returns, not every now and again. Do you tithe only now and again?
2. Giver of Offerings: As the Spirit of the Lord ministers to your heart to give offerings, do you do so? And do you give it where He directs you to give?
3. Motives: Why do you give and what do you plan on using the increase for?
4. Methods: Do you give to be seen? Are you giving grudgingly? Or out of Love?
5. What are you saying after you give: I'm broke! There they go asking for money again! It seems like just as fast as it comes in it goes out! This giving stuff doesn't work!

Or are you tithing the tithe as stated in Deuteronomy 26:1-15? Are you confessing I'm blessed going out and I'm blessed coming in, I'm even blessed in the city, suburbs wherever I go? Father, thank you for rebuking the devourer for my sake! I'm the rich protecting my riches!

6. Obedience: Are you being obedient to God even when you don't want something?
7. Holy: Are you living right 365 days a year, 7 days a week, 24 hours a day, at least to the best of your ability? And when you don't, do you repent?
8. Acting on Faith: Are you acting in Faith on God's promises, expecting Him to meet your needs? Or are you bound by fear, worry and doubt concerning your financial circumstances and situation?
9. Relationships: Do you have any unreconciled differences with a brother or sister in the Lord, or even your neighbors?
10. Greed: Are you allowing the spirit of greed to enter your heart?
11. Poor: Do you give to the poor? God says if you give to the poor you lend to him. He also says if you give to the poor you will not lack.

PRACTICAL CHECKLIST

1. Skills: Are your skills marketable and updated?
2. Employed: Are you gainfully employed? And is there truly room for growth in what you do there?
3. Work: Are you a good employee? Or do you complain, cheat on time, steal office supplies, etc.?
4. Counsel: Do you seek wise counsel? And once received, do you act on it?
5. Integrity: Are you a person of integrity?

6. Cash Management: Do you handle your money well and spend within your means? Or do you occasionally overspend?
7. Money: Do you truly understand the importance of money?
8. Plan: Do you have personal goals? Do you have family goals? Do you have a financial plan? It's been said, "If you fail to plan you plan to fail."
9. Problem Solver: Are you a problem solver? When you can solve others' problems, it often translates to income for you.
10. Income Channels: How many avenues are you giving God to funnel finances through to you? You should have at least four channels or sources of income. A picture of this is found in Genesis 2:10-15. Read the whole chapter. It speaks of the Garden of Eden, which is the perfect image for mankind and how God supplied all the needs of the Garden through four rivers. As New Covenant believers, we are the temple of God and a walking Garden of Eden; therefore, I believe we should have at least four channels or sources of income in which God could irrigate and supply our needs.
11. Save and Invest: Do you look for ways to increase your saving and investing first for the purpose of receiving more so that you will be able to give more to Kingdom business? This will also cause you to increase as seen in the parable of the three servants that received talents.
12. Spouse: How do you treat your spouse? This applies to men and women.
13. Joneses: Are you trying to keep up with the Joneses? That is, when your neighbor gets a big flat screen TV, do you get one too, knowing good and well the one you currently have is perfectly fine?

14. Slothful: The Bible tells us that slothfulness leads or tends to poverty. In fact, there were a few tribes that did not even go and get their inheritance because of slothfulness.
15. Blame: Do you blame others? Do you blame your race or the race of others? Do you blame your family tree (e.g., you didn't have a father or your mother was not the best)? Or, you don't have enough education! Or, you grew up on the wrong side of the tracks! All of these excuses may be facts, but they are not 'TRUTH' and by thinking or agreeing with them you make the Word of God have no effect. Start seeing yourself through the eyes of God and believe you are who God says you are, and you can have and do what He says you can!

Again, please note that the above list is not exhaustive and without knowing a person's specific situation, it is impossible to accurately determine the best answer. Should you want additional advice based on your specific situation, feel free to tear out the sheet in the back of the book that offers a free, no-obligation consultation and fax or mail the card to me after completing all areas that apply to you. Finally, begin everything with prayer and be honest with God. He will see to it that the Holy Spirit will give you guidance and counsel to help bring forth change.

Tithing...

Answers to Major Questions

What is tithing, and where do I tithe?

Tithing, along with giving offerings, is the method God has placed in effect for His children to prosper. When you give into the Kingdom, you are planting seed that will grow into whatever you sowed (Galatians 6:7-10). For example: Let's say you always donate your time by helping out at your local church. You will more than likely reap an abundance of time. Perhaps you will never feel tired or never be late, or maybe you will always find that people are always helping you out or visiting you.

Another example: Let's say you give finances, which in turn help the church meet its financial obligations and further various ministry efforts. In this case, you will reap financial blessings in your life. Perhaps you'll receive raises on your job when nobody else is getting raises. Or when you make purchases, it seems like there is always a sale breaking in your favor. Or maybe someone pays a bill for you. As you give to God, your heavenly Father gives back to you!

How much is a tithe?

The word tithe literally means **"tenth,"** so a tithe is one tenth of what you make. Now that you know what the amount is, the next question is where does it go? The tithe goes to "the storehouse" (Local Church), where you are being taught how to apply God's Word in every area of your life.

This should be the local church where you worship and fellowship with the saints. The key in my statement is "local church where you are being taught." You may start out giving your money to a ministry that you watch on TV—however, you should pray and believe God to lead you to a local church, because the ministry on TV, unless it's local, cannot meet your needs. An example would be if a loved one passes on and you need someone from the ministry to be at your side. How would a ministry in Ohio be able to do that if you live in Connecticut? You can support television ministry by offerings. Only you know where you are being fed the Word of God, so where you consider your storehouse to be is your decision. Just remember that you will have to give an account to the Lord as to where you place your tithes. So, you want to be sure that your tithes and offerings are always "planted into good ground."

Now, in addition to "planting" (giving)—this is something I learned from Dr. Fredrick K. C. Price—you also must keep "watering" your seed by confessing the Word and saying, "In the name of Jesus, I believe I receive the windows-of-heaven blessing." Each time you proclaim this confession, while walking in line with God's principles, you make inroads into the spirit-realm and bring your blessings forth from the spirit world into the physical world.

In the spirit world, such a confession keeps your seed (whatever you are believing and confessing) growing. When you systematically continue to make your confessions relative to your tithes and offerings, Satan cannot touch your blessings.

But when you fail to adhere to the directives given in God's word, Satan can and will steal your blessings and there is nothing God can do about it.

Further, keep in mind that, just as with seed you plant in the physical ground, there is a time element involved between planting your financial seed and receiving the corresponding harvest. God is in the spirit world, and that spirit world is outside the realm of the physical. The blessings God has given us as the result of our giving have to come from the spirit world into the physical world, and it is faith that makes that transfer. Therefore, you have to be patient. Don't be tricked into thinking that you planted today and you will reap tomorrow. Not so! Please, in the name of Jesus, don't plow your ground up. If you do that, you will most certainly miss out on your blessings. Remember that God is faithful, and He always honors His Word. Keep planting, keep watering, and your harvest is sure to manifest.

What do I do if I cannot afford to Tithe?

Many Christians have asked me this question for years. I even heard some Pastors and Ministers suggest that if you have a bill to pay and it is $100 dollars and your tithe is $90, go ahead and pay your tithes because you don't have enough anyway to pay that bill. Honor the Lord and pay your tithes! It's that kind of teaching that has the world looking at Christians as fools, and they want nothing to do with our God. To do that would be plain old **STUPID**. As a financial adviser, I always had problems hearing that kind of teaching. So I dug into the Word of God to find the truth out for myself.

As New Covenant Believers, we don't tithe because it's a law, we tithe out of LOVE. And because it's out of love, that would propel your giving beyond ten percent, especially knowing what He has done for you.

In fact, tithing is not part of the law. It was first established by Abraham **(see Genesis 14:1-24, especially 17-20).** This event happened some 300-plus years before the law was given to Moses.

When we tell a person that we are Christian and make an agreement with him to pay him for services that he renders to you, and you don't keep your word when the money is due, you have lost your witness. If you do not have enough money to pay God and pay the gas bill or any other bill for that matter, you are already overextended.

Remember, tithing is for your benefit, not God's. If you think about it, the money doesn't end up in God's hand physically. It goes to the local church, and is fed back to you in services through the church. If you have not been tithing before now, you are already a God robber, so do not start tithing until you can afford to do it. If you do not pay a bill, you are robbing the people who sent you the bill, and that is even worse than robbing God. God will forgive you, but many times, people will not.

That's why you should not read Malachi 3:10 over your offering. This verse was written to a whole nation that was robbing God, not to those of us who tithe. The scripture for tithers would be found in **Deuteronomy 26:1-19.** It's from this scripture we also learn about "Tithing." The tithe is a tenth, but once you calculated your tenth you should tithe the tenth, which requires words to be spoken out of your mouth. In other words you begin tithing the tenth.

Another thing to remember about our Father is that He looks at the heart and knows your desire to tithe. Give offerings out of love for the furtherance of the Gospel **(Luke 6:38)** and God will honor your giving. After you give with understanding, read Luke 6:38 and begin confessing,

"Thank you Lord that men/women are giving into my bosom (wallet, bank account, etc.) pressed down shaken together and running over." Once you have positioned yourself for increase, good money management is then important from this point on.

So don't spend your money foolishly, because you will certainly receive increase and will not be able to realize a difference or where it went. Once increase happens, and an individual reaches the place in his financial standing where he is meeting his obligations and can tithe without using his bill or food money, then he should begin tithing and never stop.

What is the purpose of the Tithe and who should it go to?

God's purpose for the tithes is very clear. God spoke through Malachi, **"Will a man rob God? Yet ye have robbed me. But you say, wherein have we robbed thee? In tithes and offerings....Bring ye all the tithes into the storehouse, that there may be meat in mine house..." Malachi 3:8-10.** God planned for there to be a divine sufficiency in the work of the Lord. His purpose for the tithe was to support the Levites. This is another truth that is not being fully applied in the body of Christ. This was designed because the Levites devoted themselves **solely** to their responsibility in the service of the Tabernacle; they didn't have a secular job.

When the children of Israel took possession of the Promised Land, God did not give any of the land to the Levites for their inheritance. God gave them the tithes of the children of Israel as their inheritance. God said, "And, behold, I have given the children of Levi all the tenth in Israel for an inheritance, for their service which they serve, even the service of the tabernacle of the congregation" **(Numbers 18:21)**.

So, in fact, the person that is being robbed is the priest of the house in two ways: 1) when the tithe is used for something other than his support; and 2) when it is not even tithed. Then we wonder why the people are not seeing the fullness of God's financial system operating in their lives.

The tithes of the children of Israel were distributed among the Levites and their families for their necessary food and provision so they would not be encumbered or concerned with the cares of providing for themselves or accumulating houses and lands. The tithes of the children of Israel were their only means of support.

From the tithes they received from the children of Israel, they were required to give a tithe of all they received from God as a heave offering to the Lord. God instructed the Levites through Moses, "...When ye take of the children of Israel the tithes which I have given you from them for your inheritance, then ye shall offer up an heave offering of it for the Lord, even a tenth part of the tithe." **(Numbers 18:29)**

After they presented the very best portion to God and gave it to Aaron, the High priest, (Jesus is our High priest now), the remaining portion belonged to them, their families and all their households.

God told Moses to tell the Levites, "And ye shall eat it in every place, ye and your households; for it is your reward for your service in the tabernacle of the congregation" **(Numbers 18:31).**

Now who are the modern Levites?

Ministers within the fivefold ministry, who give themselves solely to the work of the ministry, are modern day Levites. God placed apostles, prophets, evangelists, pastors and teachers within the Body of Christ for the perfecting of the saints, for the work of the ministry, and for edifying the Body of Christ **(Ephesians 4:11-12).**

Today, I believe God intends that the ministers within the fivefold ministry be supported and under-girded by the members of the Body of Christ through the giving of their tithes.

Throughout scripture you see God's plan, for the Temple or meeting place was built and maintained by offerings and the Levites were supported through tithes.

The Freewill Offering

The atonement offering of one half shekel for all males 20 years and older was used for the upkeep of the Tabernacle. Freewill offerings were used for the building of the Tabernacle in the wilderness, the Temple in Jerusalem, and later for its restoration.

God planned that there be no lack in the House of God! If every member of the Body of Christ were faithful in giving their tithes and offerings, there would be more than enough to fulfill the work of God around the world.

We would have the necessary finances now to evangelize the entire world and bring in the final end-time harvest of souls.

Where are the resources going?

Based on statistics compiled by Generous Giving, we are certainly in a position to finance the world and bring in the end-time harvest of souls. However, we as a Body have not been good stewards over God's resources and I believe a change is coming!

- In 2000, nearly 97 percent of the entire income of all Christian organizations was spent on, and primarily benefited, other Christians at home or abroad: $261 billion spent on ministering to Christians, $7.8 billion on already-evangelized non-Christians, and $0.81 billion on un-evangelized non-Christians.

- The average donation by adults who attend U.S. Protestant churches is about $17 a week.

- Among church members of 11 primary Protestant denominations (or their historical antecedents) in the United States and Canada, per-member giving as a percentage of income was lower in 2000 than in either 1921 or 1933. In 1921, per-member giving as a percentage of income was 2.9 percent. In 1933, at the depth of the Great Depression, per-member giving grew to 3.3 percent. By 2000, after a half-century of unprecedented prosperity, giving had fallen to 2.6 percent.

- Overall, only 3 to 5 percent of Americans who donate money to a church tithe (give a tenth of) their incomes, though many more claim to do so.

- Thirty-three percent of U.S. born-again Christians say it is impossible for them to get ahead in life because of the financial debt they have incurred.

Chapter 13

GOD'S SUPERNATURAL CYCLE OF PROVISIONS

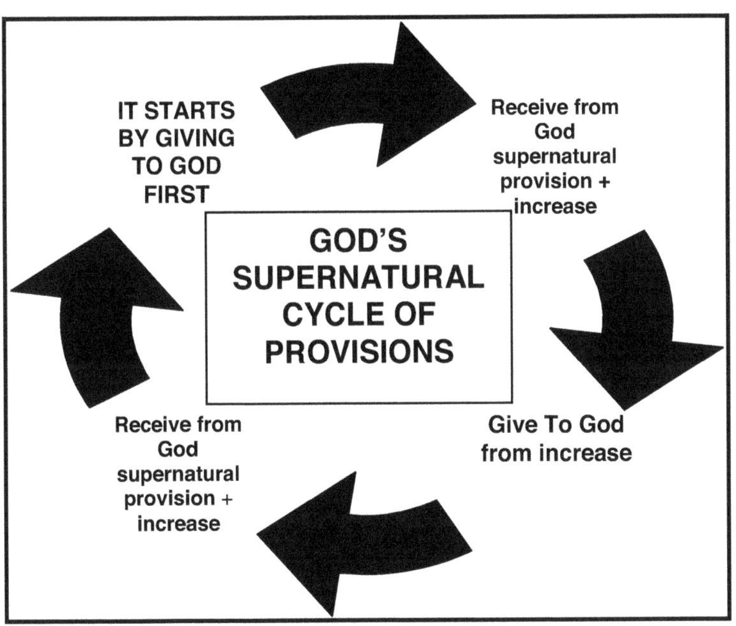

SUPERNATURAL PROVISIONS

HEBREW – "mopheth," One of the words used in the Old Testament to refer to miracles is "wonder." Translated from this Hebrew word it means "wonder, sign, portent," and is used to describe a divine act or a special display of divine power which supersedes the laws of nature. Our God is a God of signs, wonders and miracles! When He manifested His miracle-working power by delivering Israel out of Egyptian bondage, opening the Red Sea, manifesting His power and glory on Mount Sinai, raining manna from heaven, causing water to gush out of a rock, supernaturally delivering the children of Israel from their enemies and multiplying their crops, He was revealing His character as the all-powerful God of signs, wonders and miracles. God desired His people to look to Him for their supernatural provision in their lives.

GREEK – "dunamis," This word refers to the supernatural, miracle-working power of God. Through the miracles Jesus performed in healing the sick, multiplying the fish and loaves of bread, turning water into wine, casting out demons, and raising the dead, He revealed God's supernatural provision in meeting the needs of the people. The Church was born through the dunamis miracle-working power of God and through the dunamis power of the Holy Spirit that He imparted to the Church. He continues to manifest His miracle working power in supernaturally meeting the needs of His people.

God's purpose for our lives is that we live in a cycle of His supernatural provision where we are continually expecting and looking to Him to supernaturally provide our needs, and we, in turn, sow into the work of God to fulfill the great commission.

A WORD PROPHESIED OF CONTINUED PROVISION

Behold the days come, saith the Lord, that the plowman shall overtake the reaper, and the treader of grapes him that soweth seed; and the mountains shall drop sweet wine, and all the hills shall melt.

Amos 9:13

I believe we are living in that day prophesied by the prophet Amos. What this verse means to you today is that God promised to bless the work of your hands to such an extent that **"seedtime"** and **"harvest"** will overlap. God will so MULTIPLY and increase what you sow into the kingdom of God…the work of God around the world…that there will be a great ABUNDANCE in your life. The **"plowman"** will overtake the "reaper." The "seeds" you sow will MULTIPLY and grow so quickly that "harvest" will begin as soon as the seed is sown. The "harvest" of God's blessings in your life…spiritual, physical and financial…will be so great that they will last until "seedtime." There will be continual provision for your needs, and MORE! Not only will your needs be met, but God will INCREASE what you sow into His Kingdom so that you will be able to sow more. Just as God had a purpose for prospering the nation of Israel, He has a divine purpose for prospering His people today.

Chapter 14

BEFORE YOU SAY "I DO"

> And Adam said, this is now bone of my bones, and flesh of my flesh; she shall be called Woman, because she was taken out of Man. Therefore, shall a man leave his father and his mother, and shall cleave unto his wife; and they shall be one flesh.
> Genesis 2:23-24

The first institution created by God was marriage, which gave way to family. It's interesting that Father God created marriage and family before He instituted the church. The marriage institution was originally designed for both husband and wife to be co-rulers over all His creation and the earth. However, since the fall of Adam (man), the devil has used all sorts of strife and confusion to destroy the family, because he knows he will never have a family to enjoy and he wants the same for you.

One of the major areas that he attacks in the family is finances; statistics show that the number one reason for divorce is disagreements over money. If I had to pick two runner ups for divorce it would be communication and sex.

However, if we were to sum it up and get to the core, it would be money. For example, if the wife spends money regardless of how much they have or don't have without the husband knowing, he is normally going to be mad and an argument might occur. This is the result of a lack of communication, and from there the two end up not speaking for a short period of time resulting in no sexual intimacy.

During this time period when they are not speaking to each other, the devil is certainly talking to them separately. The conversation goes as such: "You know, if he really loved you, he wouldn't be upset over that little bit of money you spent. After all he bought something for himself last week!" "You mean to tell me she spent the money and she's not going to have sex with you either? Doesn't she know a brother has needs?" Then the wife gets to thinking, "Yeah that's right, maybe he doesn't really love me—after all, he compliments others more than he compliments me."

Now the husband is not only mad about the money, he is sexually frustrated and an open target for the enemy. He goes to work the next day, and the pretty receptionist from upstairs just happens to be coming in the building at the same time and they ride the elevator together alone. She compliments him, he feels good and before you know it they are having lunch and then dinner and ultimately end up having sex.

I could certainly continue with example after example, but my goal in this chapter is not to write a soap opera or solve all of the world's marital problems, and I believe you get the picture.

However, I do intend to discuss what I believe is the key issue in marriages today, which is money—or the miscommunication between two people on how to manage money.

I firmly believe that if the money issue is resolved, then half if not more marriages would stay together and I would hear from Father God, "Well done my good and faithful servant."

When the Bible in **Genesis 2:23-24** states they shall be one flesh, you have to understand God is speaking of your total being as He sees the end from the beginning. However, the first thing that becomes one is your spirits, the soul. Therefore, your mind, will, intellect and emotions are going to be a work in progress. As for your body, I believe the marriage covenant sanctioned by God brings the two bodies together as one after vows are exchanged. In fact, I would even say once the marriage is consummated during sexual intercourse your emotions are connected, too. But again, I am not going to get into a deep teaching on the marriage subject in this book. I only need to lay a foundation to point out the part that is a work in progress, which is the soul, for it is this part of the couple that creates the money problems.

Let me explain. You have two individuals who come from two different backgrounds, and in some cases two different worlds. Once you become an adult, you must know that you are a product of what you have learned or didn't learn from your parents.

Here's how it normally plays out. One person may have been taught by his/her parents to keep a budget, and from this budget spending and living are governed.

The other person may not have been taught about a budget, or perhaps he/she heard about a budget and saw the other parent disregard working within a budget, which ultimately shaped his/her thinking and values about money.

This can be identified early in the courting stage, but most of the time, emotions suppress what the intellect is trying to communicate, so the couple keeps from having such a discussion. Time elapses and they are preparing for marriage.

Deep down inside the one who was taught about a budget and lives a life within financial parameters still wants to have the talk, but it gets lost amid romance, jitters and a flurry of pre-wedding activities. That heart-to-heart review of personal finances fails to surface.

Ultimately, the budget-conscious one decided to wait for the discussion until after the marriage—after all, talking about money right before a wedding doesn't sound romantic. Of course, it takes time, and for some, it's a touchy subject they don't want to discuss. Bottom line, however, is if you can't talk about finances before the wedding, are you any more likely afterwards? Because money conflicts are a leading cause of marital strife and divorce, a candid discussion of finances before saying "I do" will go a long way in helping keep the "honey" in the honeymoon long after the honeymoon is over.

One of the first steps is often one of the most difficult, which is laying your financial cards on the table. Among young couples, this often involves the subject of debt, particularly college loans and credit cards. Each person should get a copy of his or her credit report to see if it's accurate and then share it with the other person.

Say one of you has a lot of debt and the other has none, or even has accumulated assets. Is the debt a result of necessary borrowing, such as for college or medical expenses, or is it debt accumulated by frivolous spending, poor money management or perhaps worse, something like gambling?

Believe it or not, some Christians still gamble, which is a problem in and of itself. The latter reason of frivolous spending and poor money management, however, could suggest a serious and continuing source of conflict in a marriage.

Will the person who is not in debt have assets to help pay for some of the debts, or will each party keep their finances separate, at least until the debtor has things under control? Normally, a secular adviser would suggest keeping your finances separate, but as Christians it should become the both of yours. If as a man you agree to say "I do", you are agreeing to the entire package, debt included, and you will help to pay it off as well. So, you may want to have the discussion before the wedding day.

I suggest you keep from opening any new credit lines, whether joint or not, and don't consolidate your credit reports either for it will hurt the financial strength of the other. If you are not able to come to an agreement prior to the wedding date, I suggest postponing the wedding until you clean up some of the serious debt problems.

In cases where there have been remarriages, the relationship may involve an opposite issue such as a lopsided amount of wealth, which is common today. Until now, this may have been kept secret, but it needs to be openly discussed and some advisers may suggest pre-wedding planning, such as a prenuptial agreement.

If it has not been discussed and you are about ready for the wedding, again I suggest postponing the wedding for two reasons. First, you want to be honest with each other prior to getting married. If not, the other party will always think you are hiding something, so give them a chance to prove their honesty. Second, seek the Lord now that all the cards are on the table to see if this person is the one you should marry, especially if he/she wants a prenuptial agreement.

As Christians we should not have prenuptial agreements between each other; nowhere in the Bible will you see such a thing. Many of my colleagues may disagree, but remember I started out saying this is a book written for Christians, and therefore, the Bible is always the final authority in our lives. To have a prenuptial agreement just opens the door for divorce because it brings in a root of fear. Also, how are you going to say you completely love the other person when half your goods are out of the scope of the marriage?

Beyond simply laying out your finances for the person you're going to marry, it's wise to discuss your views and beliefs about money and investing. Are you a spender, a saver, a hoarder? Does the thought of investing in the stock market make you feel uncomfortable, fearful or excited?

Which one of you will handle day-to-day finances, such as balancing the check book and paying bills?

If you have different attitudes and habits in managing money, how might you accommodate those differences during the marriage? One suggestion would be to have a joint investing goal for retirement and education, but have an agreed separate account to invest as you like.

This will work for spending differences, too. The key in my suggestion is an agreed-upon separate account, which means you both know about it, the amounts in the accounts are not kept secret, and each party has access in case of emergency.

Another point of discussion would be financial goals and dreams. You should ask each other about retirement goals, specifically when you would like to retire. What if one is looking forward to retiring at age 55 and the other is expecting to work until age 70. This may cause conflict if it's not resolved.

What if one wants to own a home, but the other wants to rent? Do you both want to have children? If you agree that children are in the forecast, then what issues might be associated with raising children, e.g., allowance, private or public schooling, and childcare.

Do you share the same philosophy about how the children's education should be paid? What of your understandings about giving to the church or to other charities?

Then you have estate planning issues, which can be very complicated when there are children from a previous marriage.

Child support issues could be a serious and explosive topic because that's essentially money made, but not coming into your house, and it affects your taxes. The bottom line here is the last thing you want are surprises after the wedding.

One of the criteria for a Christian to be married is counseling with the pastor, minister or priest before marrying. Couples also should consider talking with a Christian financial advisor.

In fact, I believe ministries should have a qualified Christian financial advisor as part of the counseling sessions and would-be newlyweds should have at least two, if not three, sessions with him/her.

However, if financial management was part of the new member's orientation, then this probably wouldn't be needed or at least could be less intense.

> Again I say unto you, that if two of you shall agree on earth as touching any thing what they shall ask, it shall be done for them of my father which is in heaven.
> Matthew 18:19

Believe it or not, talking over one's finances prior to a wedding doesn't doom it. If done properly, the wedding could be greatly enhanced, and it will certainly improve the relationship during the marriage.

Spiritually speaking, you must always remember that as believers you can go to Father God in prayer for help, and that no situation is too hard for him. Maybe you are reading this book and did not follow some of the suggestions outlined. Perhaps your marriage is under pressure as a result of financial differences and you don't know what to do. I want you to give your spouse a big hug—don't say anything just give them a big hug and repeat this for two days twice a day. During these two days, both of you should be praying for direction.

Then on the third day, schedule a time when both of you can discuss the issues. Each spouse should be prepared before the meeting to come with two or three solutions that will improve the situation.

Child of God, when you do this, understand no devil in hell will be able to destroy your family or finances because love covers a multitude of sins. Love endures, it is patient and it has a force behind it that will remove all burdens and destroy every yoke.

Then take your bills, and grab your spouse's hand, and begin to pray the prayer of agreement over your family, your finances, your children, and speak the promises of God over them and no longer speak of the things you see or speak of what appears to be defeat.

Then watch and see how God, Jesus and the Holy Spirit will get involved with your situation. Your finances will be resurrected. Remember, I said the devil is behind the strife within marriage and family because he will never have a family and his job is to keep you at odds, so don't let him win. The power of agreement is stronger than anything he could ever throw your way.

Chapter 15

OCCUPY TILL I COME

> And He called his ten servants and delivered them ten pounds, and said unto them,
> Occupy till I come.
> Luke 19:13

Occupy till I come in Luke 19:13, uses the Greek word ***"Pragmateuomai"*** (Strong's Concordance number 4231). It means **(1) to be occupied in anything, (2) to carry on a business, (3) to carry on the business of a banker or a trader.**

The second and third definitions are the ones that I would like to draw your attention to as we explore another aspect of being about our Father's business. We know Jesus himself told his parents when he was thirteen that he had to be about his Father's business. For two thousand years, we have only concluded that he meant conducting the five fold ministry. But if you ever have been involved in ministry, you know that a great part of ministry is business, and how well you handle business will determine how much ministering you will be able to do.

We also notice from Jesus' ministry that He never lacked anything, and it was a true traveling ministry so He must have handled business matters well. When they encountered times when they were unable to use the resources they had, Jesus called upon his heavenly treasure to supply supernatural resources and provision, as in the case of the feeding of the five thousand.

We also know that before public ministry, he owned and operated a carpentry business, which had to have been very successful because wherever He went people would say, "Isn't that the carpenter." In addition, some of His closest disciples were successful businessmen: Matthew a tax collector, Luke a physician, Peter a fisherman. Further, a rich man of Arimathaea named Joseph, who also was Jesus' disciple, had to go to Pilate and purchase his body for burial. Therefore, I believe Jesus' influence and success as a businessman allowed Him the ability to attract other successful business persons.

Now that your soul and spirit are open to understanding that we are called to be about our Father's business—which includes but is not limited to the five fold ministry, but rather everything we put our hands to with intention and focus—allow me to introduce two powerful concepts that we Christians must begin to embrace and strategically apply. The first is **"Moral Investing"**; the second, **"Shareholder Activism."**

Moral Investing

> Therefore, come out from their midst and be separate "says the Lord" and do not touch what is unclean; and I will welcome you.
> 2 Corinthians 6:17

Values-based investing as a concept, born as early as 1920, originally gave concerned investors the choice of avoiding investments in alcohol and tobacco. By the 1970's, the movement focus shifted from investing primarily in the above "sin" stocks to include screening for environmental pollution, nuclear power, animal rights, employee diversity, and other similar issues.

Today, morally-conscious investors can once again invest their money based on their values and screen out investments that do not line up with their faith or beliefs. Unfortunately, a growing number of public corporations appear comfortable in choosing to support or profit from a variety of immoral activities that undermine our country's traditional moral value system. In addition to alcohol, tobacco and gambling, Christians today have the responsibility and capability to also actively avoid investing in companies that are involved in abortion, pornography, anti-family entertainment, or that actively promote non-traditional married lifestyles.

By using this methodology, investors can choose to honor their moral convictions with their investments without sacrificing investment return opportunities. By being denied the use of investment capital, corporate America will learn that a financial cost is incurred for conducting business that undermines American families, moral integrity, and the institution of marriage. This is one of the core examples I believe our Lord and Savior was giving us when He said **"Occupy till I come"** in **Luke 19:13.**

FROM BOYCOTTING TO THE BOARD ROOM

As I was growing up my parents and grandparents taught me the benefit of boycotting. When we as African Americans were denied our rights, we would boycott, and this would bring public shame to the entity with hopes that they would change, and with great success most did.

Similarly, when Americans dislike a company they choose to boycott its products with the expectation that falling revenues will influence the company to change its policy. Not only did I learn from my ancestors that boycotting is a noble way of demonstrating civil rights, I later learned that it could be used to demonstrate marketplace democracy. It gives consumers the ability to vote with their dollars in an effort to cause corporate, social and/or economic change.

However, after studying the history of capitalism and the adaptation corporations made from a public relations standpoint regarding boycotting, I ultimately realized that boycotting alone is a commendable yet incomplete action. Boycotting coupled with the avoidance of stock or bond ownership of such companies is a much more effective approach. The morally conscious person has a new battlefront. By "de-funding" these companies, concerned Americans can begin voting with their investment dollars at the Wall Street level.

While pastors, ministers and the rest of the five fold ministry were teaching good Christians to avoid such things as alcohol, gambling, tobacco, pornography, ethnic disparities, and other pathologies on Sunday, they failed to realize that on Monday they were investing billions of dollars in companies that promote the very thing they were being taught to avoid.

Comparatively, the efforts of many cultural liberals, such as environmentalists, animal rights activists, homosexuals and feminists wielded their power as corporate shareholders to change corporate policy.

"And the lord commended the unjust steward, because he had done wisely: for the children of this world are in their generation wiser than the children of light."

Luke 16:8

Shareholder Activism
Our Action Plan

As a shareholder you are a part owner of a corporation. As such, you have the power to share and influence the direction of the company.

There are four components of shareholder activism, each of which is discussed below:

1. Voting your proxies on moral, social and environmental issues at annual meetings
2. Initiating dialogue with company management
3. Sponsoring shareholder resolutions
4. Divestment

VOTING YOUR PROXIES ON MORAL, SOCIAL, AND ENVIRONMENTAL ISSUES AT ANNUAL MEETINGS

When you own stock in a corporation, you have certain rights and certain responsibilities. One of the most important is the right, and responsibility, to vote. Some people may not understand the importance of a vote, whether political or corporate. Those who don't understand its importance may need to experience what it's like to be refused the right to vote. As an African American, my ancestors were refused the right to vote, so I've been taught to vote politically and corporately. Each year, companies are mandated by the Securities and Exchange Commission to send shareholders a proxy statement and a proxy ballot.

The proxy statement describes shareholder resolutions and the material facts on which shareholders will vote. The issue to be voted upon may include questions about the company's auditors, board of directors, option plan, as well as moral or social issues. Management always gives its recommendation on shareholder votes.

The proxy ballot gives written authorization for management to cast your votes at the shareholder's annual meeting. Votes are always for or against.

INITIATING DIALOGUE WITH COMPANY MANAGEMENT

Speaking with company management about issues of concern is a common technique among institutional shareholders and should become more common among believers. Talking with management avoids the confrontational approach of shareholder resolutions and may find a friendly ear.

While large shareholders such as pension and mutual funds may have a greater ability to get the attention of management, individual investors should not be stopped from voicing their concerns. Addressing a letter to the president or the investor relations department as a shareholder will most likely get a response.

As a unified body, however, we certainly have the strength to advocate moral issues grounded and rooted in biblical principles. In 2002, American evangelicals collectively made $2.66 trillion in income. Total Christian [including nominal] income in the United States is $5.2 trillion annually—nearly half the world's total Christian income, according to Mr. David B. Barrett from the World Evangelization Research Center.

SPONSORING SHAREHOLDER RESOLUTIONS

The Securities and Exchange Commission (SEC), the governmental body that oversees the stock market, has established a series of rules controlling shareholder resolutions. For individual investors there are four issues that are most important.

First, a resolution sponsor must own $2,000 (or 1%, whichever is less) of the company's stock for at least one year and must maintain this threshold level of ownership through the date of the annual meeting.

Second, a proposal for the forthcoming annual meeting must be submitted to the company at least 245 days (9 months) after the date the proxy statement was released in the previous year. Since most shareholder meetings are in the spring, they should be submitted in November or December prior to the meeting. Call the investor relations department for a firm date.

Third, the proposal and a supporting statement can be no longer than 500 words.

Fourth, the proposed resolution must pass the SEC's grounds for exclusion. For instance, the proposal cannot suggest breaking laws or rules or deal with "ordinary business" operations.

While any shareholder can become an activist, it is common for groups of shareholders to jointly agree on a resolution before it is submitted. That way, resolutions will have the best chance of receiving broad support.

DIVESTMENT

The last resort for shareholder activists is divestment, or selling stock in an offending company after attempts at dialogue or resolutions are deemed ineffective. Although divestment by an individual shareholder is unlikely to affect a corporation, many institutional investors, such as pension funds and mutual funds, can carry a lot of weight through divestment. And with the united purchasing power of the Christian community, we certainly can and should have a huge weight on moral issues; in fact, it was a command from our Lord and Savior, **"Occupy till I come" Luke 19:13.** If He told us to do it, we not only have the ability, but the promise of victory.

Chapter 16

WHO SAID YOU CAN'T TAKE IT WHEN YOU DIE?

Most believers, if not all, at one point or another have heard that famous expression, "You can't take it with you when you die!" Or how about, "Have you ever seen an armored truck behind a hearse?" These two statements imply that once you are dead it's all over and all the money you have accumulated is not going to do you any good, in hell or heaven. The purpose in this kind of preaching and/or teaching is to get the person to make a decision about their eternal salvation and accept Jesus as their Lord and Savior.

Albeit well-intentioned, in the long run, it creates a negative image about accumulating money, as well as distributing it. From a tangible asset standpoint, it is correct that you will not be able to bring your money to heaven or hell, because there is no need for currency or bartering. Jesus already paid the price for everything we need here and in heaven. He has gone before us to prepare a mansion for you and me where the streets are paved with gold and soothing music plays twenty four seven, three sixty five. As for hell, proceed with caution, for it is very hot, with no air conditioning, water, or exits. And money is not required in hell so you can leave your American Express Card at home—the bill has been covered by Satan.

From a biblical standpoint, however, it is our created purpose to accumulate wealth and riches. In this chapter I hope to share the importance of accumulating, preserving, and ultimately distributing your wealth to your children, your children's children, as well as the local church for the purpose of Kingdom building. To understand this you must first understand the word **"CHARITY".**

Traditionally, we have always defined this word as AGAPE, meaning brotherly love or the God kind of love. This is only partially correct and, therefore, has not helped you to clearly understand its use when seen in various scripture verses. Please don't get upset with me, for my goal is not to cause harm to anybody within the body of Christ. However, it is my goal as a minister of the gospel to ferret out the truth. Jesus said **"And ye shall know the truth, and the truth shall make you free." (John 8:12)** Notice He did not say tradition shall make you free, or religion shall make you free. Nor did He say your customs shall make you free. He said **"the truth shall make you free,"** so it is our job to seek out the truth.

The scripture that is most drawn upon is **1 Corinthians 13:13, which reads as: And now abideth faith, hope, charity, these three, but the greatest of these is charity.** The word charity here is "AGAPE". It literally means brotherly love, affection, good will, love, benevolence, and love feast. Most walk away believing that Paul is saying love is greater than faith when in fact he is not saying this at all.

In order to understand, you have to read chapters 12 and 13. The subject is spiritual gifts, and it is speaking of the spiritual gift of faith, not the faith that each believer received when being born again. You'll see that **1 Corinthians 12:4-10** discusses the gift of faith vs. the measure of faith dealt to every man. Then consider the following verse in Romans:

For I say, through the grace given unto me, to every man that is among you, not to think of himself more highly than he ought to think; but to think soberly, according as God hath dealt to every man the measure of faith.

Romans 12:3

Therefore, the gift of charity in its purest definition is stronger than the gift of faith, especially when you truly understand its meaning as well as its biblical application throughout scripture. You see, child of God, love as great as it is will never heal you, deliver you, put food on your table or money in your bank account, but faith will. Conversely, in order for your faith to work it must work by love. In short, love is the greatest motivator, but faith is the greatest activator.

When you see the word **CHARITY** throughout scripture, you must understand the context in which it is being used. It may mean brotherly love, affection, good will, love, benevolence or love feast. Each usage denotes a different meaning and or application. The definition most often overlooked is **"BENEVOLENCE".**

I remember going to church as a youngster with my grandmother. On the offering envelopes from her Baptist church was a place reserved exclusively for a benevolence offering.

The word benevolence is powerful. I pray you are truly focused on what the spirit of the Lord is revealing because it's going to change your life and the lives of many others through you. Benevolence literally means: Disposition to do good, an act of kindness; **a gracious gift**, a compulsory levy by **charitableness.** With this definition in mind, go back and read **1 Corinthians 13** in a King James bible. This time, read the entire chapter and insert the six specific definitions of charity, as described above, in turn, one after the other, each time the word charity appears. Then when you get to verse 13, it is summarized as the greatest of these is "AGAPE", which includes brotherly love, affection, good will, love, BENEVOLENCE, and love feast. When you flow in the gift of benevolence, you are literally giving a generous gift that is perpetual. In other words, your gift never ends, and therefore, **YOU CAN TAKE IT WITH YOU WHEN YOU DIE!**

Look at one other scripture to see how the definition of AGAPE is progressively applied.

And beside this, giving all diligence, add to your faith virtue; and to virtue knowledge, and to knowledge temperance; and to temperance patience, and to patience godliness, and to godliness, brotherly kindness and to brotherly kindness charity.

2 Peter 1: 5-7

The progression is clear from this passage of scripture. We also see the definitions of AGAPE and their progression, ending with charity, which again sums it up emphasizing what I believe, is **"BENEVOLENCE."**

There is no reason Peter would use most of the definition of agape then turn around and end by saying the same thing without mentioning the very definition that was not used, that being "benevolence." Look at one last example of this from God the Father himself, a very familiar scripture seen at baseball games and quoted by Christians and heathens all over the world, but this time, please understand its true meaning.

For God so loved the world, that he gave his only begotten son, that whosoever, believeth in him should not perish, but have everlasting life.

John 3:16

I've always known there was more to this scripture. Yes, it's powerful. I've quoted it frequently and it has brought me closer to the Lord. But in the quiet times by myself, I've always asked God how love by itself accomplishes such an enormous task. And it was not until I truly defined AGAPE, that I understood its meaning. Let us read it again with this meaning and understanding in mind. ***For God so loved the world (or showed AGAPE to the world, that is, brotherly love, affection, goodwill, love and benevolence or his disposition to do good by an act of kindness) that he gave his only begotten son (a gracious gift), that whosoever, believeth in him should not perish, but have everlasting life.***

We certainly could agree that through God's benevolence or perpetual gift of His Son Jesus, God has received more sons and daughters back into his family than could be numbered. By this compulsory levy of charitableness He was able to get everything back that was forfeited by Adam, through Jesus, who died, was buried, was resurrected and sits at the right hand of majesty.

Child of God, each time you give a generous gift, that gift allows a ministry to go on the air, feeds the hungry, clothes the naked, or gives shelter to the poor, yielding the fruit of a person accepting Jesus as their Lord and Savior. And this is a credit to your heavenly account. Please hear what I am saying—your gift of benevolence plays a key role in spreading the gospel, reaping the harvest of souls even in your absence, and Father God credits each soul won from your gift to your account. It is also perpetual because that person will share the gospel with someone else, bringing salvation to them and that person will share it with another person, and then that person will do the same, and so on and so on.

BENEVOLENCE IS THE "PERPETUAL GIFT"
IT LITERALLY HAS NO END....

Our estates are made up of assets plus income, which equals the total financial capital of a person. You may choose to direct your estate at death or you may choose by default to allow the government to do so. If you fail to plan, the money will be directed at death by the government to the social needs of our country. But if you properly plan, you can direct your estate to your family and the social needs of your choice. Our churches and other non-profit organizations fill many of America's social needs and, therefore, the government allows for taxes to be reduced when directing your assets to them. By employing techniques to direct your estate, you can actually increase the size of your estate for your heirs, benefit the church or other non-profit entity, and help society all at the same time.

Professional advisors are largely silent on the topic of charitable planning. I believe some of the reasons that generous giving is given little attention by professional advisors include:

1. **The fear of losing money, because client giving might decrease an advisor's total amount under management;**

2. **The fear of coming across as nosy or invasive, and thereby alienating clients, and;**

3. **The belief that religious or philanthropic issues are outside the bounds of financial planning.**

As Christians, we are charged with the responsibility of spreading the gospel and making disciples. This is done with the use of buildings, television, radio, tapes, books, CDs, internet and missions. And all of this requires finances. Many churches, after decades of operation, do not have on reserve at least three months of operating expenses. This is usually due to poor financial management, not from misappropriation of funds—that is, not maximizing the money given and/or not creating vehicles for people to properly give beyond tithes and offerings.

A gifting program should be a part of every church and church leaders should make such a program widely known and easily executed. This would result in more money being generated for the Lord's work.

Many churches have different accounts, such as operating, missions, programs, etc. Churches should also establish a special fund that works in the same manner as a foundation.

Below you will find some information that I believe will help you better understand estate planning and gifting strategies, including two of my personal favorites, "Family Foundations" and "PSEUDO Foundations." And remember, a charitable gift of "BENEVOLENCE" is perpetual and a credit to your account from God, therefore, **YOU CAN TAKE IT WHEN YOU DIE!**

WHAT KEY ESTATE PLANNING TOOLS SHOULD I KNOW ABOUT?

Planning is a part of nearly everything we do in life. It's even a part of dying. How will you preserve your assets from estate taxes and probate fees? How will you ensure distribution according to your wishes? Who will make financial and medical decisions in the event of your incapacity?

By taking steps in advance, *you* have a greater say in how these questions are answered. And isn't that how it should be?

Wills and Trusts

Wills and trusts are two of the most popular estate planning tools. Both allow you to spell out how you would like your property to be distributed, but they also go far beyond that. Just about everyone needs a will. Besides enabling you to determine the distribution of your property, a will gives you the opportunity to nominate your executor and guardians for your minor children. If you fail to make such designations through your will, the decisions will probably be left to the courts. Bear in mind that property distributed through your will is subject to probate, which can be a time-consuming and costly process.

Trusts differ from wills in that they are actual legal entities. Like a will, trusts spell out how you want your property distributed. Trusts let you customize the distribution of your estate with the added advantages of property management and probate avoidance. Wills and trusts are not mutually exclusive. While not everyone with a will needs a trust, all those with trusts should have a will as well.

Durable Power of Attorney for Finances

Incapacity poses almost as much of a threat to your financial well-being as death does. Fortunately, there are tools that can help you cope with this threat.

A durable power of attorney is a legal agreement that avoids the need for a conservatorship and enables you to designate who will make your legal and financial decisions if you become incapacitated. Unlike the standard power of attorney, durable powers remain valid if you become incapacitated.

Health Care Proxies and Living Wills

Similar to the durable power of attorney, a health care proxy is a document in which you designate someone to make your health care decisions for you if you are incapacitated.

The person you designate can generally make decisions regarding medical facilities, medical treatments, surgery, and a variety of other health care issues. Much like the durable power of attorney, the health care proxy involves some important decisions. Take the utmost care when choosing who will make them.

A related document, the living will, also known as a directive to physicians or a health care directive, spells out the kinds of life-sustaining treatment you will permit in the event of your incapacity. The directive creates an agreement between you and the attending physician.

The decision for or against life support is one that only you can make. That makes the living will a valuable estate planning tool. And you may use a living will in conjunction with a durable health care power of attorney. Bear in mind that laws governing the recognition and treatment of living wills may vary from state to state.

Estate Planning Tip

Keep all your important financial and legal information in a central file for your executor. Be sure to include:

- letters of last instructions
- medical records
- bank/brokerage statements
- income and gift tax returns
- insurance policies
- titles and deeds
- will and trust documents

How Can My Charity and I Both Benefit from My Gift?

One popular estate planning technique is planned giving. Making a donation to a qualified organization provides some very attractive benefits.

You could receive an immediate income tax deduction. With a properly structured gift, you could realign your investment portfolio without paying capital gains tax on appreciated property. Another strategy may allow you to pass your estate on to your children while avoiding both probate and estate taxes.

To Whom Can You Give?

You're free to give your property to whomever you choose. To retain the tax advantages associated with planned giving, however, your gift must be made to a qualified organization. The vast majority of donations are made to charitable organizations. To qualify, a charitable organization must have been organized in the United States, be operated on a strictly non-profit basis, and not be politically active.

In addition to common charitable organizations, you may give to veterans' posts, certain fraternal orders, volunteer fire departments, and civil defense organizations.

What Can You Give?

You can contribute almost anything to a qualified organization. The deduction limits are more restrictive for gifts other than cash, but you are free to give almost any property of value.

What Are the Gifting Strategies?

In addition to making an outright donation, there are a number of different gifting techniques you can use. For example, you can give life insurance. This enables you to give a large future gift at a relatively modest cost.

A charitable remainder trust allows you to retain an income interest in a future gift. With a charitable lead trust, you can give the income to the charitable organization and retain the principal for your heirs.

What Are the Benefits?

Making a planned gift can provide some significant benefits. A charitable contribution may qualify you to receive a significant current income tax deduction.

Your deduction for an outright gift will equal the value of your gift up to certain generous limits. You can carry forward any gift amount that exceeds these limits for up to five years.

With a charitable lead trust, you can pass an appreciated asset onto your heirs with little or no estate taxes.

By using a charitable remainder trust, the Trustee can sell highly appreciated gifted investments and reinvest the proceeds to generate income without paying capital gains tax. Thus, a properly planned gift could enable you to realign your investment portfolio without incurring any current income taxes. That could allow you to diversify your holdings and even increase your cash flow.

The only thing you can't do is take back your gift. You can't start selling assets and then pocket the money. But you can change the charity that will eventually receive your gift.

Whatever gifting strategy you choose, planned giving can be very rewarding. It's wonderful to see your gift at work and to receive tax benefits as well.

**The information provided here is to assist you in planning for your future. Any analysis is a result of the information you have provided. Proper tax and legal advice should always be obtained.*

WHAT GIFTING STRATEGIES ARE AVAILABLE TO ME?

There are a number of different gifting strategies available for planned giving. Each has its advantages and disadvantages. Instead of making an outright gift, you could choose to use a charitable lead trust. With a charitable lead trust, your gift is placed in a trust. The recipient of the gift draws the income from this trust. Upon your death, your heirs will receive the principal with little or no estate tax.

If you prefer to retain an income interest in your gift, you could use a pooled income fund, a charitable remainder unitrust, or a charitable remainder annuity trust. With each of these strategies, you receive the income generated by your gift, and the recipient receives the principal upon your death.

Finally, you could purchase a life insurance policy and name the charitable organization as the owner and beneficiary of the policy. This would enable you to make a large future gift at a potentially low current cost.

The following chart summarizes the advantages and disadvantages of various gifting strategies.

Gift	Advantages	Disadvantages
Outright Gift	Deductible for income taxes	No retained interest
Charitable Lead Trust	A current gift to charity Current income tax deduction Pass assets to heirs at a future discount	Transfer of assets is irrevocable If current income tax deduction is taken, future income is taxable to donor Donor gives up use of income for life of the trust
Pooled Income Fund	Income tax deduction Income paid to beneficiary for life Non-income-producing assets can be converted to income-producing assets	Income is unpredictable from year to year Income received is taxed as ordinary income Remainder interest will usually go to only one charity
Charitable Remainder Unitrust	Current income tax deduction Avoids capital gains tax on appreciated property Reduce future estate taxes	Transfer of assets is irrevocable Qualified appraisal generally required Complex administration and setup

Charitable Remainder Annuity Trust	Income tax deduction Avoids capital gains tax on appreciated property Fixed income	Fixed payment cannot be limited to the net amount of trust income Qualified appraisal generally required Complex administration and setup
Gifts of Insurance	Current income tax deduction possible Enables donor to make a large future gift at small cost in the future	May require annual premiums In some cases the death benefit could be part of donor's taxable estate

THE CHARITABLE REMAINDER TRUST

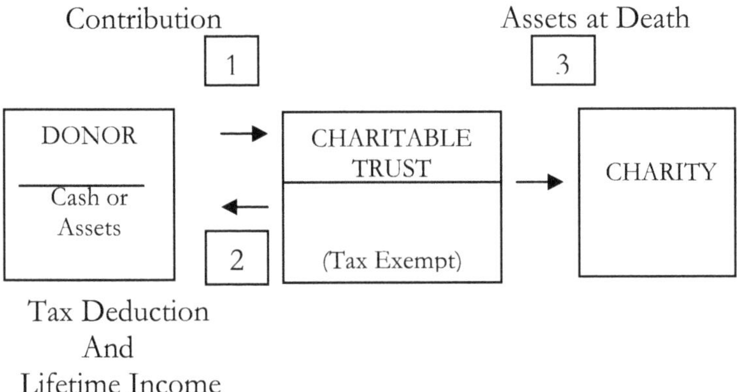

How Can I Benefit from a Wealth Replacement Trust?

Charitable giving can be a rewarding experience by allowing you to both give and receive. To enjoy the benefits of charitable giving, you can utilize a variety of strategies.

The Basics of Charitable Remainder Trusts

To establish a charitable remainder trust, you transfer appreciated property to an irrevocable trust and designate the charity of your choice as the beneficiary of the trust. The property within the trust is then sold and reinvested to provide income. You retain a lifetime interest in the income generated by the trust, and when the trust expires at your death, the property within the trust is transferred to the charitable organization.

You are entitled to a current income tax deduction for the charitable gift, subject to certain limits. And because the property was sold within the charitable trust, you will not have to pay tax on any capital gains. This enables the full value of your property to be reinvested, which will increase the income generated by the trust. It also enables the charity to receive a larger gift.

If you have heirs, charitable remainder trusts have one major drawback: When the charitable trust terminates, the property within the trust is transferred to the charitable organization—rather than to family heirs. So while the charitable remainder trust offers many benefits, this strategy can effectively disinherit your heirs.

Replacing Gifted Assets

One effective solution to this situation is the wealth replacement trust.

To create a wealth replacement trust, you use a portion of the income from a charitable remainder trust to buy a life insurance policy.

You decide how much of the charitable gift to replace. You can buy enough insurance to replace only a portion of the property that will eventually pass to charity, or you may prefer to replace all of the property within the charitable remainder trust.

The wealth replacement trust is often designed so that upon the death of the second spouse, the death benefit of the life insurance policy goes to your heirs. These funds replace the property that passes to the charity from the charitable remainder trust. And because the life insurance policy is owned by the trust, the proceeds of the policy will generally not be subject to estate taxes at either death.

An Appropriate Strategy?

If this strategy sounds interesting to you, there are a variety of considerations. The cost and availability of life insurance depend on factors such as age, health, and the type and amount of insurance. Before implementing this strategy, it would be prudent to have the policy approved. In addition, you should seek professional advice from an attorney before establishing such a trust. In many cases, the wealth replacement trust is an appropriate way to preserve family wealth.

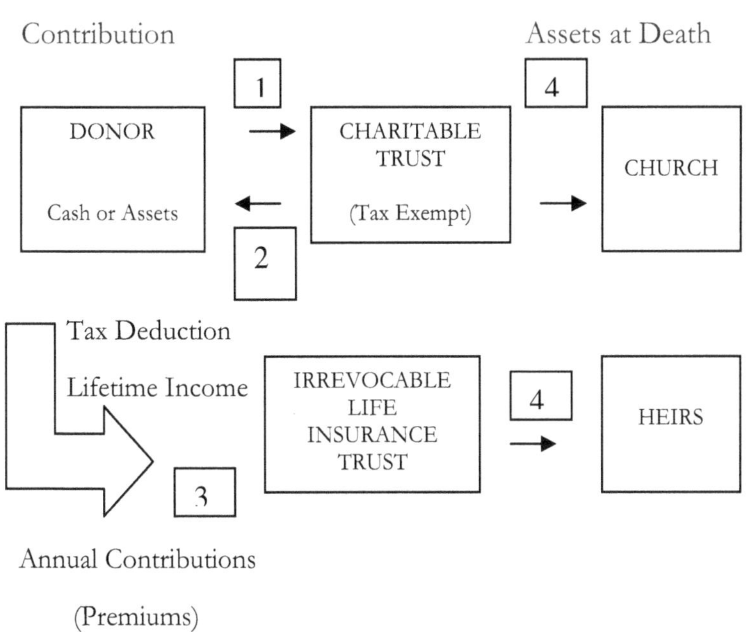

TITHING AT YOUR DEATH

Most Christians never ponder the question of whether and how they should tithe at their death. The truth of the matter is that we are responsible to tithe at our death—it is not enough to merely tithe during our lifetime. It is commonplace for a person to accumulate more wealth in a person's estate than during their lifetime. The sources of this wealth in their estate could be:

1) **Life Insurance benefits**
2) **Sale of homes and other real estate**
3) **Sale of family businesses**
4) **Liquidation of IRAs, 401 (k) plans and investments**
5) **Sale of tangible assets**

We all know that ten percent of our income is to be given to the Kingdom while living, but a tithe is also required on the accumulation of one's wealth from income earned over a lifetime. By simply putting together a plan and writing a direction into your will or trust, you can direct ten percent of your estate to benefit the Kingdom and world evangelism.

When you tithe at your death, it doesn't necessarily have to deplete your estate to make the gift. The above wealth replacement trust strategy can be used to make sure your heirs receive their inheritance—while ensuring the church or other non-profit also benefits. Further, you may even increase the estate if properly structured.

Remember that through careful planning, you can ensure that the wealth you've accumulated here on earth will reap perpetual benefits for the Kingdom, long after you've gone.

Roll-over IRAs and Distributions

ROLL-OVER IRA FAQs

Q. **What is a Rollover IRA?**

A. A Rollover IRA is a type of Individual Retirement Account that is often used by people who have changed jobs or retired and have assets accumulated in their employer-sponsored retirement plan.

Eligible distributions from such plans can be rolled over directly into your own personal Rollover IRA without incurring any tax penalties and assets remain invested tax-deferred. Consolidating multiple employer-sponsored retirement plan accounts into a single Rollover IRA can make it easier to allocate and monitor your retirement assets.

Q. **How long does it take to roll my retirement plan assets to my own Rollover IRA?**

A. A rollover is made up of three steps: Opening a Rollover IRA account with a financial institution, contacting your former employer(s) or the manager of your former employer's plan and providing what they may require to process the distribution, and moving the money into your new Rollover IRA. Note that if you have an existing Traditional IRA at this institution, you can roll your assets into that account. Your trusted financial advisor will be able to help you with this.

Q. **Will I be better diversified by keeping my money in more than one place?**

A. Portfolio diversification comes from spreading your money out over different kinds of investments, including stocks, bonds, real estate, and cash, which generally reduces risk without sacrificing potential returns. If your retirement plan offers several different kinds of investments, you will have more options for staying diversified within your account. However, diversification does not ensure a profit or guarantee against loss.

Q. **Can I roll over assets into my Traditional IRA?**

A. Yes. If you choose to roll additional assets into a Traditional IRA, your ability to roll these assets to a new employer's retirement plan in the future depends on what that plan allows. If you were born before 1936 or if you are rolling assets from a 457(b) plan, there may be additional tax considerations. Contact your tax advisor for more information.

Q. **Will I owe taxes on my Rollover IRA?**

A. There are two ways to roll over your assets from your former employer-sponsored retirement plan to a Rollover IRA or Traditional IRA, and the tax implications may be different depending on which you choose to do.

Direct Rollover: In this situation, the distributions go directly from your employer-sponsored retirement plan to the IRA via a trustee-to-trustee transfer.

60-Day Rollover: You can withdraw your former employer-sponsored retirement plan assets and then roll them over into your own Rollover IRA. You must complete the rollover within 60 days of receiving the distribution to avoid current income taxes. You will be subject to a mandatory 20% withholding for federal income tax, which you would have to replace if you want to roll over your entire distribution to your own Rollover IRA. If you hold the assets for more than 60 days, your distribution will be subject to current income taxes and a 10% early withdrawal penalty if you are under age 59½ .

Both ways will allow your assets to continue to grow tax-deferred until withdrawal.

Consider keeping your Rollover IRA funds separate from your Traditional IRA assets if you anticipate investing your Rollover IRA assets in another employer-sponsored plan in the future.

For more information on your options when you receive a retirement plan distribution, visit my website at: www.NCFALLC.com. Click on Learning Center, then click articles or email me at: HJW@ncfallc.com.

Q. **Can I move an existing IRA from one institution to another?**

A. Yes. There are two methods.

Direct (custodian-to-custodian) Transfer: By completing a transfer of Asset Form in addition to a new IRA Account Application from the new institution, you will be authorizing the new institution to accept the transfer of your IRA from the other institution to your new account with them. Your trusted financial advisor will be able to help you with this.

You may want to hold Rollover IRA funds separately from Traditional IRA assets so that you have the flexibility to roll over your Rollover IRA assets in a new employer-sponsored plan in the future.

60-Day Rollover: You can withdraw your IRA from the other institution and roll it over to your new IRA. You must complete the rollover within 60 days of receiving the distribution to avoid income taxes and, if you are under age 59½, the 10% IRS early-withdrawal penalty. Only one rollover is allowed per IRA in any 12-month period. You will be subject to a mandatory 20% withholding for federal income tax, which you would have to replace if you want to roll over your entire distribution to your own IRA later.

RETIREMENT PLAN DISTRIBUTIONS

Q. **Can I roll over the distribution check my former employer's plan administrator sends me?**

A. Yes, but if your former company plan makes the check payable to you, 20% of your eligible retirement plan distribution will be withheld for federal income taxes.

The only way to avoid this withholding is to have your former employer's plan administrator make your distribution check payable to the financial institution you've chosen as custodian for your new IRA. Either you or your former employer's plan administrator should then send this check directly to the financial institution.

Q. I already received a check made payable to me and 20% was withheld. If I roll over my money now, can I get that 20% back?

A. You'll have to replace the 20% that was withheld with your own savings if you want to roll over your entire distribution to your own IRA—all within 60 days of receiving the distribution. If you do, the 20% that was withheld is credited toward your income tax liability when you file your tax return. However, if you don't have the cash to make up for the 20% withheld, the IRS will consider that 20% as a distribution, making it subject to taxes and a possible 10% early withdrawal penalty if you are under age 59½ .

Q. Can I roll over all the money in my former employer-sponsored retirement plan account?

A. Yes. You can roll over all the contributions made to your plan and any earnings on those contributions that haven't yet been taxed (referred to as pre-tax contributions). If you made contributions to your plan with income that had already been taxed (referred to as after-tax contributions), you can roll over those assets as well.

To determine how much of your contributions and earnings were pre-tax versus after-tax, review the statements you received, or ask your current employer's benefits office for assistance. It is your responsibility to keep track of after-tax contributions on IRS Form 8606. Consult your tax advisor if you have questions.

Q. Can I move my former employer-sponsored retirement plan assets into a Roth IRA?

A. Roth elective deferrals can be rolled into a Roth IRA. Or, if eligible, you can convert a Rollover IRA or Traditional IRA to a Roth IRA.

Assets that can be converted to a Roth IRA include deductible and non-deductible contributions to a Traditional IRA, earnings or appreciation of those contributions, and any eligible assets rolled over to the IRA from other retirement plans. Learn more about Roth IRAs by visiting my website at www.NCFALLC.com. Click on Learning Center and read the applicable articles.

Beginning in 2008, the Pension Protection Act of 2006 will allow for direct rollovers from qualified employer-sponsored retirement plans to Roth IRAs for eligible individuals.

Q. What if I need my former employer-sponsored retirement plan money to pay for living expenses?

A. Depending on your situation, you may want to roll your retirement plan assets into a Rollover or Traditional IRA. If you need money to pay for expenses, you can always withdraw what you need, when you need it.

A withdrawal from an IRA is subject to ordinary income tax, and may be subject to a 10% early withdrawal penalty if you are under 59½. Minimum required distribution must begin by April 1st of the year following the year in which you turn 70½. Ask your tax advisor if there are any circumstances which would cause your distribution to be eligible for special tax treatment, such as a financial hardship.

Q. Can I add more money to my Rollover IRA later?

A. Yes. You can add money to your Rollover IRA either with annual contributions or additional employer-sponsored retirement assets. Some people choose to make their annual contributions to their Rollover IRA so that they only have to keep track of one account. This may be right for you if you have no desire to roll these assets back to a qualified retirement plan at a future employer. Assets can be co-mingled and still be eligible to roll into another employer plan in the future; however, it is at the discretion of the receiving plan to determine what type of assets can be rolled over.

Q. Can I leave my former employer-sponsored retirement plan assets in my current plan indefinitely?

A. No. Generally, you must begin to take withdrawals, known as required minimum distributions (RMDs), from all your retirement accounts (excluding Roth IRAs) no later than April 1st of the year following the year in which you turn age 70½. Check with your former employer to see if additional restrictions exist or learn more about calculating RMDs.

Q. What is Net Unrealized Appreciation (NUA)?

A. When a lump-sum distribution of company stock is taken from a retirement plan, ordinary income taxes are due only on the cost basis of those securities, not the current fair market value. The difference between the cost basis and the current fair market value, or the Net Unrealized Appreciation (NUA), is taxed only when the securities are sold and only at the lower long-term capital gains tax rate.

Q. When is a Net Unrealized Appreciation (NUA) strategy favorable?

A. For participants who own employer stock that has grown in value from their original cost, it may be beneficial to adopt a NUA strategy for the employer stock. From a tax perspective, it is generally more favorable for the participants to roll over retirement plan assets to an IRA or new employer-sponsored plan rather than take a lump-sum distribution. For participants who have large amounts of appreciated company stock, however, it may be more beneficial to take a lump-sum distribution of company stock instead.

Hypothetical Examples:
An individual owns 1,000 shares of company stock with a current fair market value of $80,000. An individual paid $20 per share for a cost basis of $20,000. An individual's Net Unrealized Appreciation is $60,000 ($80,000-$20,000).

If an individual adopts an NUA Strategy and takes a lump-sum distribution of the employer stock, he/she will owe income tax on the $20,000 (plus a 10% premature distribution penalty if he/she is under age 59½). Assuming a 25% federal tax, 5% state tax, and 10% premature distribution penalty, the individual would pay $8,000 in taxes for the year of the lump-sum distribution. The $60,000 of appreciation would not be taxed until the securities were sold and would only be taxed at the then-current long-term capital gains rate, which is currently 15%. Any additional appreciation from the original distribution date would also only be taxed at the long-term capital gains rate.

If an individual elected to roll over the company stock to an IRA and then eventually take a distribution, even if after age 59½, an $80,000 distribution would result in a $24,000 tax bill in a single year (assuming a 25% federal tax rate and a 5% state tax rate).

NUA Guidelines

You must take a lump-sum distribution of all assets in the plan to qualify. You may elect, however, to roll over the non-employer stock securities to an IRA for continued tax-deferred growth.

The employer stock must be moved in-kind from your plan to a brokerage account (i.e., keeping the same investments).

You must hold the employer stock for at least 12 months in the brokerage account until you are eligible for long-term capital gains rates.

To preserve your retirement savings, it may be advantageous to pay the taxes due on the cost basis from another source of money.

Q. What if I'm married then begin contributing to my retirement plan and end up several years later getting a divorce. Is my spouse entitled to any of my retirement assets?

A. Yes. The law states that he/she is entitled to half of your assets unless there was a prenuptial agreement or a waiver of their rights to such assets. For specific rollover instructions of assets and tax liabilities resulting from a divorce decree, please consult your legal advisor, trusted financial advisor, and tax advisor.

8
MOST COMMON ANNUITY MYTHS

Only 42 percent of U.S. workers have tried to determine how much they will need to save for a comfortable retirement according to Employee Benefit Research Institute, 2005. Further, about half of Americans spend more time planning for their annual vacation than thinking about retirement funding, according to Boston Globe, November 6, 2005.

So, what do we think, say, and do with our money? Too often, we base our thoughts, phrase our words, and take action based on myths that have been passed down from parent to child, sibling to sibling and friend to friend. Regardless of what you read or whose opinion is being sited for or against annuities, they certainly are critical to the retirement process, but yet there are more myths circling this investment than possibly any other investment.

I believe it is safe to say all professionals, authors and TV personalities agree on one thing, and that is that people are living longer. Social security is going to have a different look and employers are not going to take care of you. Therefore, a retirement plan that is well funded is vital. The key is which vehicle to use to achieve such funding goals—mutual funds, annuities or stocks and bonds. As you plan, you can pretty much bank on some financial advisor recommending an annuity.

The truth of the matter is, in some cases, annuities make sense and in others they do not. But you don't want to base your decision on a myth; nor do you want to be duped! Remember, in all your getting, get understanding.

Before discussing what an annuity is, the different kinds of annuities or even how they work, I want to deal first with the *myths*. I believe it is more important to debunk the myths about annuities so the proverbial scales can be removed allowing you to see clearly. Then, you will be ready to learn what and how these investments may help you on your road to financial freedom.

MYTH ONE
"Annuities are prohibitively expensive."

One persistent myth is that variable annuities are dramatically overpriced and simply cost too much. The fact is, their many unique benefits often justify any incremental costs, and variable annuities are often not significantly more expensive than other investments.

Annuities are long-term, tax-deferred vehicles designed primarily for retirement. As contracts with insurance companies, annuities can provide valuable death benefit protection for your heirs should you die prematurely, or provide you with guaranteed income options regardless of how long you live. Plus, today's unbundled annuities can be custom-built so you only pay for features and benefits that are important to you.

So, are the benefits worth the price? You can ask the same question about health or homeowner's or other insurance. You really don't know until you have a claim, and you probably don't want to take a chance and find out. The same is true with retirement and insuring your future or your loved ones in your absence.

Further, if options like tax-deferred growth potential, tax-free exchanges, income guarantees and death benefits for your heirs are appealing, then a variable annuity might be right for you.

REALITY

Variable annuities offer a variety of benefits, which many investors find worth the costs.

MYTH TWO

"Annuities are not good investments because gains, when withdrawn, are taxed at higher ordinary income tax rates than other investments."

A common misconception is that annuities have less attractive tax rates than other investments that are subject to long-term capital gains rates. The reality is that the long-term tax treatment is much more favorable than many people might believe, plus tax-deferred annuities have the added potential to accumulate significantly more than vehicles which may be subject to taxation each year.

On the surface, gains withdrawn from annuities are taxed as ordinary income with rates as high as 35% (revised for JGTRRA 2003). But that's not the whole story.

We have a progressive income tax system in the United States. In theory, that means the more income you make the higher the tax rate you pay. However, our system actually blends all the rates as you move up the scale. For example, a married couple, filing jointly, and earning $59,400 to $119,950 (2005), will pay between 13.8% and 19.4% on their earnings.

The blended rate depends on their actual income within the range. At the top of the range, they'll be close to 19.4%, but far less than the 28% marginal rate. So with an annuity, you're really not talking about a vehicle taxed at 35%.

Additionally, people tend to focus strictly on the effect of taxation during the income stage, without considering the substantial advantage of tax-deferral. Many investments are taxed annually. Therefore, when the tax bill is paid from the account, the assets are reduced each year and your income could also be reduced. Because annuities are not subject to annual taxation, they can provide greater potential asset growth over time, and the dollars that otherwise could go to pay taxes remain in your possession. Of course, at the time withdrawals are taken, taxes will be incurred on untaxed earnings.

So when you break it down, greater potential for tax-deferred accumulation coupled with a blended tax system can translate into a significant advantage.

Please note: The tax rate for long-term gains is currently 15% or 5%, depending on income.

REALITY

The effective tax rates on variable annuities are seldom as high as you might think.

MYTH THREE

"If a trust owns an annuity, then the annuity loses its tax deferral treatment."

Many people mistakenly believe that when a trust owns an annuity, the tax deferral benefit is automatically forfeited. While the rules under 72(u) do prohibit the tax-deferred treatment for non-natural owners, that's not the whole story. In fact, trust-owned annuities may be able to retain the tax-deferral benefit. Since 1986, Private Letter Rulings have been used to clarify when an annuity owned by a trust may still receive the tax-deferred treatment. And those rulings generally hinge on the beneficial owner concept.

In a nutshell, if the beneficial owner of the trust is a person, then the tax-deferred treatment of the annuity has generally stood. And it makes sense. Annuities are long-term vehicles for retirement, and 72(u) usually denies tax-deferred treatment for non-natural beneficial owners. However, a trust can generally retain its tax-deferred treatment if you can establish that the trust's beneficial owner is a person.

Hakeem J. Webb and National Christian Financial Advisors do not provide legal or tax advice. For questions about a specific situation, please consult a qualified tax adviser or reach our firm directly for estate planning help via email at hjw@ncfallc.com or by phone at 1-866-540-3129.

REALITY

A trust, based on previous Private Letter Rulings, can potentially be able to retain its tax-deferred treatment if the beneficial owner is a person.

MYTH FOUR

"Annuities are treated the same way as other assets when inherited."

The tax treatment of an annuity at the owner's death is often misunderstood. Many people believe that because annuities don't receive a step up in basis at death, they create a negative tax liability. In actuality, annuities can have advantages over other investment types.

Annuities are subject to estate and income taxes, and the beneficiary is liable for income taxes. To alleviate the treatment of double taxation, the Internal Revenue Code provides an income tax deduction to the beneficiary, called the Income in Respect of the Decedent, or IRD. This provision allows the beneficiary to deduct the estate taxes, paid by the estate, on his or her income taxes. The deduction can only be claimed as an itemized deduction.

To clarify this potential advantage, let's consider a hypothetical example. Suppose Mark has amassed an estate worth $3 million, which consists of a $1 million annuity that was originally purchased for $100,000. Upon Mark's death, his estate will be subject to a maximum 46% estate tax rate.

Mark named his son Matthew, age 50, as the beneficiary of the annuity. Matthew is in the 28% income tax bracket. Matthew is eligible to take an income tax deduction on the IRD, which is subject to annual adjusted gross income (AGI) limitations for itemized deductions. The ability to use the full deduction is limited by the annual threshold, which is adjusted each year.

If Matthew exceeds this threshold, his ability to use the full deduction will be reduced. To maximize the deduction, Matthew will have to carry it forward into future years. Matthew needs the continued tax deferral and future income more than he needs an immediate lump sum distribution, so he decides to stretch the distributions and is thus required to take a distribution of $30,000 in the first year following Mark's death.

Matthew's AGI for that year is under the AGI phase-out threshold (using 2006 rates), including the distribution, and his taxable income is $95,000, resulting in his incurring a 2006 income tax liability of $20,931.50. Over the period that he receives annual distributions, his income tax liability will be $252,000 based on the $900,000 IRD.

Matthew's payout option provides for gains from the annuity to be paid out first, then the principal after that. He is therefore entitled to an income tax deduction equal to the amount of estate tax paid on the IRD that he received.

The result is his receiving an income tax deduction in that first year of $13,800, reducing his income tax liability to $17,067.50 from $20,931.50 and providing income tax deductions over the life of the stretch distributions totaling $414,000 on the $900,000 IRD.

*Investors should take into consideration possible changes to tax laws, the impact of inflation and other inherent risks when making decisions regarding distribution options.

REALITY

Annuities, when inherited, can have advantages over other investments.

MYTH FIVE

"Annuities provide no additional value when held by a qualified plan or an IRA."

Many people argue that qualified money doesn't belong in individual annuities. The main reason cited is that you end up paying for the benefit of tax deferral. Nothing could be further from the truth. Annuities do not, in fact, charge for tax deferral, regardless of whether it is qualified or not-qualified. The tax-deferred status inherent in annuities is actually a result of longstanding federal law. And while the benefit of tax-deferred growth may be duplicated, the benefit actually costs the investor nothing.

It is important to note that annuities may not be appropriate for qualified money if the only benefit of the product is tax deferral, nor are they intended for short-term investors, or where required minimum distributions will result in a withdrawal charge.

However, annuities may be appropriate for qualified plans when the other benefits, such as lifetime income payments, family protection through the death benefit and guaranteed fees, support the recommendation.

And, it is important to bear in mind that variable annuities, both qualified and non-qualified, are fee efficient for those who want a variety of investment options from professional portfolio managers and believe in rebalancing their portfolios without incurring a tax liability each year. How much benefit has been derived from the death benefit option?

The National Association for Variable Annuities (NAVA) reports that VA death benefits paid out in 2003 exceeded the cash value of those contracts by more than $1.2 billion! Anyone who says that qualified money does not belong in an annuity most likely does not understand annuities, including the additional advantages they can provide. Keep in mind this figure does not factor in death benefits from fixed or equity index annuities, just variable, so the total number for all annuities is even higher.

REALITY

"The living and death benefits offered in annuities may provide reason to invest qualified assets in them." According to Cerulli Associates, 2001. Cerulli Associates is a Boston-based research firm specializing exclusively in the financial services industry.

MYTH SIX

"You can add more money to a 72(t) or 72(q) program in order to change the income amount."

A common misconception is that by adding money to a 72(t) or 72(q) program, you can increase the annual amount received. This is simply false.

As many investors are aware, Internal Revenue Codes 72(t) and 72(q) allow individuals to make penalty-free withdrawals from their former employer-sponsored retirement plans. The regulations were established to ensure that individuals with a serious need for income before age 59½, such as a layoff or an early retirement situation, would have the flexibility to remove money from their retirement plans without paying the 10% federal tax penalty.

There are, however, a few important stipulations. To remove money and avoid the penalty, withdrawals must be made in substantially equal periodic payments, which cannot be altered until age 59½ or for at least five years. One of the most common misunderstandings is that by adding money to the retirement account, either through transfers, exchanges or rollovers, you can increase the amount withdrawn each year. But the revenue codes clearly forbid this sort of material modification, insisting instead that such transactions void the individual's exception provided in Internal Revenue Codes 72(t) and 72(q). Once voided, you can expect to owe the 10% federal tax penalty on the entire amount withdrawn in the tax year the exception is voided. Understanding this myth can save you a big IRS headache!

REALITY

Adding funds to a retirement account with an existing 72(t) or 72(q) program voids the individual exception.

MYTH SEVEN

"An IRA beneficiary's beneficiaries can stretch the balance over their own life expectancies."

Another common belief is that an IRA beneficiary's beneficiary has the same distribution options as the original beneficiary. Certain options remain the same, such as lump-sum payment. However, the ability to stretch death distributions over his or her life expectancy is false. Only the original beneficiary has this ability.

Let's consider a hypothetical example. At age 60, Paul purchased a non-qualified annuity. Paul passed away in the beginning of 2002, at the age of 75. The death benefit on Paul's annuity was passed to his 40-year old son, Timothy, as beneficiary.

Because Timothy did not need the money in the account for his own retirement needs, he elected to stretch the benefits of his father's annuity over his 43.6 year life expectancy*. Timothy was also able to name a new beneficiary and decided to name his two daughters, Esther and Sarah.

Upon Timothy's death at the end of 2028, assuming current tax laws, his two daughters want to stretch the benefits again, but this time as the beneficiaries of a beneficiary, they are not able to use their own life expectancies.

After considering possible changes to tax laws, inflation, and other risks, both elect to continue the distributions through their father's life expectancy, thus reducing the impact of taxes, until the period has expired in the year 2045.

The stretch concept is designed only for investors who will not need the money in the account for their own immediate retirement or other financial needs.

REALITY

Death distributions can only be stretched over the original beneficiary's life expectancy.

MYTH EIGHT

"Death benefits are not worth the money."

Some contend that the price of death benefits is too high. Those who have inherited more money than they would have without the benefit might disagree. The reality is that death benefits provide an opportunity to add value to annuity contract proceeds.

All annuities provide a guaranteed minimum death benefit, usually the greater of contributions paid into the contract or the contract value at death. For example, if an annuity owner contributed $200,000, never withdrew any money, and it is only worth $150,000 at death, the beneficiary would receive the full $200,000.

The value of this benefit cannot be overstated, particularly in light of the bear market from 2000 to 2002. And if history is any guide, and it's the only guide we have, it is safe to say we will experience another down market, but history also lets us know that after such down markets the markets are punctuated with historic gains. Nevertheless, the individual who purchased an annuity and died during such time just insured for their loved ones at least the amount invested and potentially more. This would not be true in any other investment.

Another death benefit often uniquely available to annuity owners is the step up. This feature, usually offered at an additional cost, locks in investment gains, if any, so that annuity investors can be confident that their beneficiaries will receive a stepped-up amount. Of course, if the contract value is greater than the death benefit, their beneficiaries will receive the contract value.

REALITY

Death benefits can add value to annuity contracts, while giving the investor and his/her family peace of mind to invest slightly more aggressively.

What is an Annuity?

An annuity is a periodic payment intended to begin at either a specific or to-be-designated date, or lasting for either a fixed period or for a period measured by a designated life or lives. Withdrawing funds too rapidly will exhaust retirement savings and could lead to impoverishment. Withdrawing funds too slowly will lower the retiree's standard of living and could produce an unintended windfall for heirs. By pooling the resources of many individuals, the life annuity provides a stream of income that cannot be outlived.

COMPARED TO LIFE INSURANCE

Annuities and life insurance both provide protection against a loss of income. By creating an estate, life insurance provides protection against dying too soon (i.e., a premature death). In contrast, by systematically liquidating an existing sum of money the annuity provides protection against living too long.

QUALIFIED ANNUITY VS. NONQUALIFIED ANNUITY

A "qualified" annuity is one that is used as part of a qualified retirement plan that complies with the provisions of Code section 401(a). In contrast, a "nonqualified" annuity is not associated with an employer-provided qualified retirement plan and may be purchased by any individual or entity. Despite its name, a "nonqualified" annuity offers unique tax advantages. The following writings of annuities relate to nonqualified annuities.

PARTIES TO AN ANNUITY

As with a life insurance contract, there are a number of parties to an annuity who acquire different rights and obligations under the annuity contract.

[1] Owner

Every annuity contract must have an owner, who is also referred to as an "annuity holder." The owner does not have to be an individual person, but can be a trust or other legal entity. The internal cash value buildup of an annuity is not currently taxable, unless the contract is owned by a corporation or other entity that is not considered under the tax law to be a natural person.

The annuity contract owner has essentially the same ownership rights as the owner of a life insurance contract.

Under the annuity contract, the owner names the individual who will serve as the annuitant, names the individual or entity, who will be the beneficiary under the contract, determines when the contract will be annuitized, and has the power to make partial withdrawals from the contract or fully surrender the contract for its cash value.

[2] Annuitant

The annuitant is that individual named in the annuity contract whose life serves as the measuring life for purposes of determining benefits to be paid under the annuity contract. In this sense, the annuitant under an annuity contract is comparable to the insured under a life insurance contract. Unlike the owner and the beneficiary, the annuitant must be an individual.

Annuity contracts can have more than one annuitant (e.g., a contract providing a joint and survivor benefit to husband and wife has two annuitants). While it is most common for the owner and annuitant to be the same person, they can be different (e.g., a father purchases an annuity and makes his 45-year-old son the annuitant in order to use his son's life in calculating benefit payments).

[3] Payee

This is the person who receives the annuity payments. Most often the payee is also the owner and annuitant, but the payee can be merely the owner, with another individual as the annuitant.

[4] Beneficiary

Should the owner, or under some circumstances the annuitant, die after premiums are paid but before the contract is annuitized (i.e., begins paying out benefits), a death benefit allows for recovery of the amount invested in the contract. The beneficiary is that individual or entity who is named to receive this death benefit. However, the **beneficiary** typically has no other rights under the contract.

[5] Insurance Company

An insurance company issues commercial annuities to the annuity owner, whereas private annuities are contracts between individuals. In the annuity contract the company undertakes certain financial obligations to the owner, the annuitant, and the beneficiary.

THE ANNUITY MATRIX

The annuity Matrix below will provide a better understanding of the basic features of the nonqualified annuity. These features include but are not limited to:

[1] How Purchased

Annuities can generally be purchased by paying installment premiums that are typically level periodic payments, by a single premium, or by flexible premiums, which allow premiums to be made at varying intervals and in varying amounts.

[2] When Payments Begin

When payment is made with a single premium the purchaser has the choice of beginning payments immediately (an immediate annuity) or deferring payments until a later date (deferred annuity).

[3] How Funds Are Invested

The individual purchasing an annuity can choose between annuities offering a variety of guarantees and investment options.

Fixed Annuity

The term "Fixed annuity" refers to the interest rate paid by the issuing company on the annuity contract. Despite its name, this rate does change. During the accumulation phase a fixed annuity provides a current rate that is subject to change after an initial guarantee period typically ranging from one to five years. A minimum guaranteed rate is also provided.

Fixed annuity contracts containing a bailout provision allow the contract holder to withdraw funds without a surrender charge if the credited interest rate falls below a specific bailout rate. The premiums paid for a fixed annuity become part of the insurer's general account and the purchaser has no say as to how they are invested. Once annuitized the contract pays a periodic fixed dollar amount.

Equity-Indexed Annuity

The equity-indexed annuity (EIA) is a hybrid of the fixed and variable annuities. By linking the interest rate to an equity index the EIA allows the contract holder to benefit from the returns associated with a rising stock market. A minimum guaranteed interest rate provides protection from a falling stock market. Any professional offering such investment to you does not need a securities license to sell EIAs because they are considered to be fixed-rate annuities.

Variable Annuity

A variable annuity allows the owner to select from among a number of investment options, to include various mutual funds, bond funds, money market accounts, and a guaranteed account (also referred to as a "fixed" account). Under federal law the variable annuity is considered a "security" and therefore subject to a much higher degree of regulation than the fixed annuity. Any professional offering you a variable annuity must have the required securities licenses and a prospectus must be delivered with or preceding a proposal to a prospect or client. Therefore, make sure you inquire whether the professional has the appropriate license.

During **the accumulation phase,** variable annuity premiums are placed in separate accounts that are held and invested apart from the insurance company's assets held in the general account. (While not precisely the same, the separate variable accounts are also referred to as sub-accounts, variable sub-accounts, flexible accounts, and flexible sub-accounts). As an investment option, most variable annuities offer a guaranteed account, also referred to as a fixed account, which functions much like a fixed annuity.

Subject to both timing and dollar limitations, the holder of a variable annuity is allowed to periodically transfer funds between separate accounts, and between separate accounts and the guaranteed account. This investment flexibility allows the account holder to reposition investments in response to market conditions or due to a desire to either increase or decrease risk (e.g., as retirement age approaches amounts might be transferred out of stock sub-accounts and into the guaranteed account).

An **accumulation unit,** also referred to as a unit of credit, is the measure used to track the value of a variable annuity during the accumulation phase. As additional premiums are paid, the annuity holder is credited with additional accumulation units. The values of these units fluctuate according to the values of the underlying investment accounts.

When a variable annuity is **annuitized** the contract's **accumulation units are exchanged for annuity units.** The number of annuity units received depends not only upon the existing accumulation units, but also upon the insurance company's assumptions regarding mortality, dividend rates, and expenses; therefore, make sure your trusted advisor is representing more than one choice to you. In calculating the number of annuity units, the insurance company uses an assumed interest rate (AIR) that, if earned, will produce a level benefit payment.

Some annuity contracts allow the contract holder to select an AIR within a narrow range of rates. By opting for a lower AIR the conservative contract holder accepts fewer annuity units, and lower initial dollar payments, in exchange for an increased likelihood of increasing benefit payments (in an up market) and a decreased likelihood of decreasing benefit payments (in a down market).

Once annuitized, the number of annuity units remains constant but the dollar amount of the annuity payments will fluctuate depending upon the investment results of the underlying assets. Thus, the annuity holder who elects payments under a variable option is subject to the risk that monthly benefit payments may decrease as well as increase.

[4] Forms Of Payment

Under the settlement options, also referred to as payout options, the annuity owner has a contractual right to take payment of the annuity proceeds in a number of ways.

Withdrawals from an annuity can be either partial or full, or made under a systematic program providing for periodic income. Although partial or full surrenders may be subject to contract fees or surrender charges, particularly in the early years of a contract, under most annuity contracts systematic withdrawals are made without these charges.

Systematic withdrawals typically take one of three forms; **interest only, flat dollar amount, or an amount based upon a calculated life expectancy.**

Because they avoid annuitization of the contract, systematic withdrawals provide the contract owner with a great deal of flexibility to withdraw more or less funds as needed. Withdrawals are subject to ordinary income taxes and possible penalty taxes imposed by the IRS.

An **annuity certain** involves payment of a fixed amount or sum without regard to the **life-expectancy** of the annuitant or annuitants.

Payments for a **fixed period** allow the payee to receive the annuity's accumulated value over a set number of years. This is similar to the fixed payments that are received under an installment sale. A variation of the fixed period, known as a temporary life annuity, provides for the payments to terminate should the annuitant die before the end of the fixed period.

Payments for a **fixed amount** allow the annuitant to receive set benefit payments for **as long as the annuity's accumulated value lasts.**

A **life annuity** involves payment of a periodic income for a period of time **measured by the life of the annuitant or annuitants. One or more** individuals may be named as the annuitants under a settlement option.

A settlement option involving a single life annuity is the simplest and purest form of assuring a stream of income that cannot be outlived. Benefits are paid for the life of a single annuitant, with all payments ceasing upon the annuitant's death. Settlement option can also involve multiple lives. Virtually all multiple life annuities involve two individuals, but in theory it is possible for annuities to cover any number of lives (the following discussion assumes two lives).

A **joint life annuity** provides for payments so long as both annuitants are alive. However, all payments terminate upon the death of either of the annuitants. There is limited demand for this type of annuity settlement option.

A **joint and survivor annuity,** also referred to as a "joint and last survivor annuity," provides for benefit payments during the joint lives of two individuals. This is clearly the most popular form of annuity settlement option, particularly when the annuity is issued to provide a retirement income to a husband and wife.

Under a full joint and survivor annuity the surviving annuitant continues to receive the same amount as was paid before the first death. This amount continues to be paid until the deaths of both annuitants, at which time all payments cease.

Under a joint and two-thirds survivor annuity the surviving annuitant receives payments equal to two-thirds of the full amount that had been received by both annuitants. This reduced amount continues to be paid until the death of the surviving annuitant, at which time all payments cease.

The traditional form of this annuity distinguishes between the individual designated as the principal annuitant and the individual designated as the secondary annuitant. Payments to the secondary annuitant are reduced by one-third if the principal annuitant dies first, but there is no reduction in payments to the principal annuitant if the secondary annuitant dies first. The more popular contemporary form of this annuity reduces payments to the survivor no matter which annuitant dies first.

Under a joint and one-half survivor annuity the surviving annuitant receives payments equal to one-half of the full amount that had been received by both annuitants. This reduced amount continues to be paid until the death of the surviving annuitant, at which time all payments cease. A reduction in payments to the surviving annuitant may depend upon which annuitant dies first.

[5] Guaranteed Minimums

Contract holders are often reluctant to accept a contract that could result in a loss of all values upon the untimely death of an annuitant or annuitants. Because of this, insurance companies offer settlement options that provide for minimum returns.

Refund guarantees assure that if the annuitant (or annuitants) dies before receiving cumulative monthly payments equal to the annuity's purchase price, the beneficiary will receive the difference between the annuity's purchase price and the cumulative payments received by the annuitant (i.e., the unrecovered portion of the purchase).

Most often, these refunds guarantee repayment of the entire purchase price, but some variations provide for lesser amounts (e.g., a 50% refund annuity). Refund guarantees are offered with contracts covering a single life and joint life annuities that terminate on the first death, but refund guarantees are not likely to be found with joint and survivor annuities.

Lump sum refunds, also referred to as cash refunds, make one single payment to the beneficiary.

Installment refunds continue periodic payments to the beneficiary in the same amount as paid to the annuitant, until such time as the cumulative payments equal the purchase price.

Period certain guarantees, also referred to as a "life annuity certain" and "life annuity with installments certain," assure that if the annuitant (or annuitants) dies before receiving a stipulated number of payments, the remaining guaranteed payments will be made to the beneficiary. Under this option, the insurance company is promising to pay the annuity benefit for the longer of the annuitant's lifetime or a certain number of years. Most contracts offer guarantee periods of 5, 10, 15, and 20 years, but other durations are found.

[6] Accumulation Phase vs. Distribution Phase

It is important to recognize that single premium annuities and flexible annuities have two distinct phases. The accumulation phase is that period of time from the purchase of the annuity until the annuity holder decides to begin receiving benefit payments under the annuity. The distribution phase, also referred to as the liquidation or annuitization phase, is that period of time beginning with the first periodic benefit payment under the annuity (i.e., when the contract is "annuitized").

Contract holders will often elect different forms of annuities between the accumulation and distribution phases (i.e., a single premium deferred variable annuity is initially purchased, but is later annuitized after the accumulation period as a fixed annuity providing a guaranteed monthly income).

[7] Fees and Charges

When comparing annuities it is most important to determine the impact of fees and charges, particularly with regard to the projected returns on variable annuities. These fees and charges can include:

[a] Investment management fees ranging from 0.25% to 1% or more.

[b] Administration expense and mortality risk charges ranging from a low of maybe 0.5% to a high of 1.0% or more.

[c] Annual maintenance charges are often not assessed, but average $50.00.

[d] Fund exchange charges by variable annuities are generally waived on a limited number of exchanges per year, but can range up to $10 per transaction once you exceed the limit.

[e] Surrender charges vary between companies and policies but are typically phased-out over a period of 4-10 years. Due to competition, new products are entering the market place with lower surrender charges than ever before and some products offer as little as a one year, known as a "C" share product.

In conclusion, and most importantly, there is much to learn about annuities and, more often than not, they are misrepresented by the media, critics, and some financial professionals who aren't even licensed to offer them. As we've seen, there are reasons why annuities sometimes are not suitable for an investor. But there are even more reasons why they sometimes make sense, especially with the new guaranteed minimum death benefits (GMDBs) and the various living benefits, which in many cases have actually replaced the traditional selling points of death benefits.

Indeed, when you take into account the new living benefit riders, such as guaranteed minimum withdrawal benefits (GMWBs), guaranteed minimum accumulation benefits (GMABs) and guaranteed minimum income benefits (GMIBs), these newer products are a blend of investments and insurance and they are meeting a need and covering a risk of major importance, known as **"longevity risk".**

The U.S. Census Bureau's July 2002 report estimated over 76,000 centenarians in America that year, and projected the number to rise to 129,000 in 2010. The longer life expectancies of our population pose an important question: Will you have enough money to last and allow you to live the standard of life you've been accustomed to living?

Glossary – Asset Classes

Large Cap, Value: A domestic equity category of portfolios holding primarily large capitalization stocks (market capitalization over $5 billion) with market valuation that are lower than the market average (based upon measurements such as price-to-earnings ratio, price-to-book, and price-to-cash flow).

Large Cap, Growth: A domestic equity category of portfolios holding primarily large capitalization stocks (market capitalization over $5 billion) with market valuations that are higher than the market average (based upon measurements such as price-to-earnings ratio, price-to-book, and price-to-cash flow).

Mid Cap Equity: A domestic equity category of portfolios holding primarily stocks with market capitalization between $1 billion and $5 billion.

Small Cap, Value: A domestic equity category of portfolios holding primarily small capitalization stocks (market capitalization under $1 billion) with market valuations that are lower than the market average (based upon measurements such as price-to-earnings ratio, price-to-book, and price-to-cash flow).

Small Cap, Growth: A domestic equity category of portfolios holding primarily small capitalization stocks (market capitalization under $1 billion) with market valuations that are higher than the market average (based upon measurements such as price-to-earnings ratio, price-to-book, and price-to-cash flow).

International Equity-Developed: An international equity category representative of portfolios holding stocks of developed countries such as Japan, Australia, and those in Western Europe. Additional risks (i.e., currency fluctuations, political changes, marketability) are associated with international investing.

International Equity-Emerging: An international equity category for portfolios focused on emerging or developing economies. Additional risks (i.e., currency fluctuations, political changes, marketability) are associated with international investing.

Short Term Government Bonds: A domestic fixed income category for portfolios focused on government bonds, Treasury bills and notes, GNMA, FNMA, CMOs and other agency debt of typically 1 to 3 years maturity.

Intermediate Term Government Bonds: A domestic fixed income category of portfolios focused on government bonds, Treasury bills and notes, GNMA, FNMA, CMOs and other agency debt of typically 3 to 7 years maturity. This guarantee is applied to the underlying bonds and applies only to the timely payment of principal and interest. The value of the government bond itself will fluctuate with changes in market conditions so when redeemed or sold, you may receive more or less than the amount originally invested.

Long Term Government Bonds: A domestic fixed income category of portfolios focused on government bonds, Treasury bills and notes, GNMA, FNMA, CMOs and other agency debt of typically 10 years or longer maturity. Government bonds are made up of bonds that are guaranteed by the government and/or a government agency. This guarantee is applied to the underlying bonds and applies only to the timely payment of principal and/or interest.

The value of the government bond itself will fluctuate with changes in market conditions so when redeemed or sold, you may receive more or less than the amount originally invested.

Glossary – Key Terms

Corporate Bonds: A domestic fixed income category of portfolios focused on investment grade (BAA or higher) corporate and utility bonds. The value of the underlying bonds will fluctuate with changes in market conditions so when redeemed or sold, you may receive more or less than the amount originally invested.

High Yield Bonds: A domestic fixed income category of portfolios focused on non-investment grade (BA or lower) bonds. The value of the underlying bonds will fluctuate with changes in market conditions so when redeemed or sold, you may receive more or less than the amount originally invested.

International Bonds: An international fixed income category of portfolios which includes corporate and government bonds. Additional risks (i.e., currency fluctuations, political changes, marketability) are associated with international investing.

Municipal Bonds: A domestic fixed income category of portfolios focused on municipal bonds. The value of the underlying municipal bonds will fluctuate with changes in market conditions so when redeemed or sold, you may receive more or less than the amount originally invested.

Fixed Annuity: An insurance category which includes single premium, fixed annuities, and equity-index. A new category within the fixed annuity are index annuities.

Real Estate Securities: A domestic equity category of portfolios emphasizing tradable real estate-related securities, such as real estate investment trusts (REITS).

Precious Metals: A domestic equity category of portfolios investing in companies which engage in mining, distribution, and/or processing of precious metals.

Cash & Cash Equivalents: A money market category which includes all cash type vehicles, such as CDs, money market funds, bank accounts, Treasury Bills (T-Bills), etc. CDs are federally insured (to $100,000 per account) and offer a fixed rate of return. The principal and interest of investment alternatives to CDs, on the other hand, can fluctuate with changes in market conditions. Therefore, when these instruments are redeemed or sold, you may receive more or less than the amount originally invested. T-Bills and government bonds are guaranteed by the government as to the timely payment of interest and principal only. The market value of the T-Bill and/or government bond itself will fluctuate with changes in market conditions. Therefore, when these bonds are redeemed or sold, you may receive more or less than the amount originally invested.

Additional Contributions: Refers to anticipated cash inflows.

Asset Allocation: The process of determining what proportions of your portfolio holdings are to be invested in the various asset classes.

Asset Class: A standard term which broadly defines a category of potential investment.

Asset Mix: The percentage weightings (or mix) of different asset classes to be held in the portfolio. There may be separate asset mixes for the taxable and tax-deferred holdings in a portfolio. The composite asset mix represents the total combination of taxable and tax-deferred holdings.

Current Dollars: A forecast of the asset value stated in terms of the actual dollars held, not in terms of purchasing power.

Efficient Frontier: Plots the asset mixes, ranging from conservative to aggressive, that provide the best trade-off of risk and return. These "efficient" asset mixes provide (1) the maximum available assumed return for a given level of risk, and (2) the minimum available level of risk for a given level of assumed return.

Financial Goals: Refers to anticipated cash outflows.

Inflation Dollars: A forecast of the asset value measured in terms of purchasing power. Because of inflation, investment dollars will probably not be able to buy as much in the future as they can today.

Risk: The unpredictability of investment returns. The chance that the actual return from investment in an asset class will be different from its assumed return. Risk is measured statistically using standard deviation. Other forms of investment risk exist. Investors should reference specifically the risk disclosure section of each prospectus.

Sharpe Ratio: A measure of incremental assumed return (in inflation dollars) provided by an asset class of asset mix for taking additional risk. Higher values of the Sharpe Ratio are desirable.

Standard Deviation: A statistical measure of estimated average annual investment risk. It is the possible divergence of actual return from its estimated total return. It measures the potential magnitude for any positive over performance or negative underperformance. There is a 68% probability that the actual return will fall within one standard deviation of the estimated total return. There is a 95% chance that the actual return will be within two standard deviations.

Total Return: The combined return in current income and capital appreciation from investment in an asset class.

Yield: The current cash income received from investment in an asset class. Bonds provide yield in the form of interest payments and stocks through dividends.

FOUR COMMANDMENTS FOR THE RICH & ANOINTED

Commandment No. 1 – Do not be arrogant.
(1 Timothy 6:17)

Commandment No. 2 – Do not put your hope or trust in your riches.
(Proverbs 23:5, Psalm 62:10)

Commandment No. 3 – Be rich in good deeds.
(Deuteronomy 8:18, Galatians 6:10, Ephesians 6:8)

Commandment No. 4 – Be liberal and generous-hearted; eager to share.
(Ecclesiastes 5:13)

NOW THE RICH MAN'S CHARGE

I will never be high-minded.

I will never trust in uncertain RICHES.

I will keep my trust in The Living God.

I will always enjoy my blessings from God.

I will always be ready to distribute when God calls upon me.

In the name of Jesus Christ.

Salvation Prayer

Salvation is a gift that is made available to those who repent, believe and confess that Jesus is Lord and that He died and rose from the dead to save mankind **(Acts 16:31; Romans 10:9-10)**. This gift cannot be earned through good deeds or by simply being "good" **(Ephesians 2:8; 1 Timothy 1:9)**. It is a matter of faith (acting out on what you believe according to God's Word concerning salvation).

If you have come here looking for a change in your life, if you have come seeking a peace that is found only through a personal relationship with a loving God, then you are at the right place. God is ready and willing to help you—right now, and right where you are.

Pray this prayer:

Heavenly Father, I come to You in the Name of Jesus. Your Word says, "Whosoever shall call on the name of the Lord shall be saved" **(Acts 2:21)**. I am calling on You. I pray and ask Jesus to come into my heart and be Lord over my life according to **Romans 10:9-10**. "If thou shalt confess with thy mouth the Lord Jesus, and shalt believe in thine heart that God hath raised him from the dead, thou shalt be saved." I do that now! I confess that Jesus is Lord, and I believe in my heart that God raised Him from the dead.

Additional Resources

If you have prayed this prayer, welcome to the family of God! We would like to send you some materials that will help you to get started on your new walk with the Lord! So please either call us at: 1-866-540-3129, or visit us on the web at www.NCFALLC.com. On the home page, click on the "contact us" tab and then complete the form. In the comment section, mention that you just prayed this prayer and received Salvation. You can also email us at: hjw@ncfallc.com.

Remember!

II Corinthians 8:9

For ye know the grace of our Lord Jesus Christ, that, though he was rich, yet for your sakes he became poor, that ye through his poverty might be rich.

About The Author

As the CEO and C0-founder of National Christian financial Advisors, (NCFA), I bring over 15 years of services, retail and institutional wealth management experience to your ministry or family. The principal focus of NCFA is to help The Body of Christ create, preserve, and distribute wealth for their families and heirs by developing and maintaining long-term relationships through excellence, faith, integrity and exceptional client satisfaction. We provide Bible based investment consulting services and deliver wealth management planning and 401(a), 403(b) and 401-K designs and management solutions to Ministries, Pastors, Municipalities, families, individuals and high net worth individuals. NCFA has access to global equity and debt markets, mortgages, and banking products.

Hakeem, is also a wealth management consultant with CFD Investments and an Investment Advisory Representative of Creative Financial Designs, Inc.. Hakeem began his professional career with Equitable Co., Inc., currently AXA Advisors, as a Product/Marketing analyst. Then he specialized in developing and setting up retirement plans for small to midsize companies, public schools, universities, municipalities, churches and nonprofit organizations. Subsequently, he held a Financial Consultant position with Fleet/Natwest Brokerage, overseeing roughly $25 million in investment assets.

Hakeem received his M.S. Degree in Financial Services from The Institute of Business and Finance. In addition, he has various designations from several industry groups. These designations include: Board Certified in Mutual Funds, Certified Annuity Specialist, Certified Fund Specialist, Certified Senior Consultant and Retirement Income Specialist. He taught Financial Management classes and conducted leadership training sessions at Norwalk Community College and is a much sought after conference speaker.

PERSONAL

He is a lifetime member of Full Gospel Businessmen International. He is a Minister at Abundant Harvest Outreach Ministry in New Haven, Ct (Pastor Curtis Antrum); Loan Committee Member of Waterbury Economic Development; Economic Development Chair for NAACP State Conference Connecticut; Member of The Quinnipiack Club in New Haven, CT.; Recently selected to serve on the IBF Standards Committee. Most importantly, he is married to Beverly and have four lovely children--Elijah, Emmanuel, Victoria and Isaiah.

"GIFT OF APPRECIATION" I would like to personaly thank you for buying my book! As a token of my appreciation please complete this form and select ONE of the COMPLEMENTARY NO OBLIGATION SERVICES A $200.00 DOLLAR VALUE AND MAIL THIS FORM BACK TO OUR OFFICES.

__Retirement Income Analysis
__College funding Analysis
__401-K Investment Allocation Review
__Portfolio Moral Audit
__Consultation for a church building expansion
__ Other ____________

Name ____________
Home Address ____________
City ____________ State ________ Zip Code ________
Home Phone ____________ Work Phone ____________
Employer ____________ Position ____________
Address ____________
Best time to call: ________ a.m. ________ p.m. Email address:________

1.866.540.3129
Hakeem J. Webb, MSFS, RIS
NCFA, Inc.
49 Leavenworth Street
Suite 305
Waterbury, CT 06702
VISIT US ON THE WEB AT: www.NCFALLC.com

www.ingramcontent.com/pod-product-compliance
Ingram Content Group UK Ltd.
Pitfield, Milton Keynes, MK11 3LW, UK
UKHW020133250726
13967UKWH00002B/618